# SOCIOLOGY OF EDUCATION SERIES

Gary Natriello, Series Editor

*Advisory Board:* Jomills Braddock, Sanford Dornbusch, Adam Gamoran,
Marlaine Lockheed, Hugh Mehan, Mary Metz, Aaron Pallas, Richard Rubinson

Mandating Academic Excellence:
High School Responses to
State Curriculum Reform
BRUCE WILSON and
GRETCHEN ROSSMAN

Who Chooses? Who Loses?:
Culture, Institutions, and the
Unequal Effects of School Choice
Edited by BRUCE FULLER and
RICHARD F. ELMORE with GARY ORFIELD

Hosting Necomers: Structuring
Educational Opportunities for
Immigrant Children
ROBERT A. DENTLER and
ANNE L. HAFFNER

# From the Series Editor

With growing numbers of immigrants entering the country, the United States is confronted once again with the challenge of incorporating newcomers into American society. A primary vehicle for this process is the public school system. Although the public schools have always played a role in incorporating newly arriving students, their role is more important than ever before at a time when a high school diploma is the minimum requirement for successful participation in economic life. In this volume Robert Dentler and Anne Hafner examine the responses to immigrant children offered by twelve school districts in the southwest. Although each of the districts is faced with substantial numbers of immigrant students, they differ markedly in their capacity to facilitate the academic progress of these students. The authors uncover the key elements of successful approaches to meeting the educational needs of recently arrived students.

Several features of the study merit special mention. First, although the authors examine operations in individuals schools, the focus of the analysis is on the school district as the unit that determines the reception that immigrant students will receive. The leadership of the district and the deployment of resources within the district are critical issues in framing the responses to immigrant children. Second, by focusing on school districts, the authors are able explicitly to link the differing capacities of these twelve districts to the demographic characteristics of the communities in which they are embedded. For each district, the analysis includes a detailed account of the social and political forces within the community that constrain or empower the efforts of the local schools. Third, by selecting districts that differed in their ability to enhance student performance, not in the absolute levels of student performance, Dentler and Hafner focus squarely on the capacities of districts to promote student progress.

This volume illustrates how sociologists of education are able to employ distinctly sociological perspectives to shed light on problems of contemporary educational practice. By combining approaches that illuminate the operation of district organizations with approaches that take into account the larger community context, the analysis yields a multiply layered explanation of the factors that lead to disparate outcomes for newcomer students. The understandings derived from the analysis are expressed in terms of concrete policies and practices that can be considered by others interested in enhancing the educational experiences of immigrant children.

*Gary Natriello*

# HOSTING NEWCOMERS

*Structuring Educational Opportunities for Immigrant Children*

Robert A. Dentler
Anne L. Hafner

Teachers College, Columbia University
New York and London

To Helen Hafner, a wonderful mother and teacher
—A. H.

Published by Teachers College Press, 1234 Amsterdam Avenue, New York, NY 10027

A preliminary version of this book was prepared at the Southwest Regional Laboratory under a subcontract to Far West Laboratory from the U.S. Department of Education, the Office of Educational Research and Improvement (Contract #003-3450). The opinions expressed in this publication are those of the authors and do not necessarily reflect the views of the supporting agency.

*Library of Congress Cataloging-in-Publication Data*

Dentler, Robert A., 1928–
    Hosting newcomers : structuring educational opportunities for
immigrant children / Robert A. Dentler, Anne L. Hafner.
        p.      cm. — (Sociology of education series)
    Includes bibliographical references (p.   ) and index.
    ISBN 0-8077-3613-9. — ISBN 0-8077-3612-0 (pbk. : alk. paper)
    1. Children of immirgants—Education—United States.
    2. Immigrants—Education—United States.  I. Hafner, Anne L.
    II. Title.  III. Series: Sociology of education series (New York,
    N.Y.)
    LC3746.D46   1997
    371.826'91'0973—dc21                                        96-50969

ISBN 0-8077-3612-0   (paper)
ISBN 0-8077-3613-9   (cloth)

Printed on acid-free paper

Manufactured in the United States of America

04 03 02 01 00 99 98 97   8 7 6 5 4 3 2 1

# Contents

# Foreword

These are the newcomers, those children and adolescents who arrive in the United States accompanying parents or other relatives or by themselves, running away from political chaos, famine, persecution, perennial unemployment, or in search of a way of life which allows some freedom of choice. They suffer a special kind of trauma, one from which they will probably never fully recover.

Newcomers arrive at an unknown culture, are faced with an unknown language. The change is sudden and dramatic. Nothing could have adequately prepared the young newcomer for what he or she would find here. Those who studied English suddenly realize they don't know enough to communicate the simplest thoughts. Those who had mastered algebra find themselves doing long division two grades below as a newcomer in a public school. Some who have never learned how to read and write are assigned to a freshman English course their first day in high school because there's no more room elsewhere. The school itself is a strange new experience, as is the bus, P.E., and, of course, the cafeteria. The students inhabiting the strange-looking halls act differently and dress differently from those at home.

Newcomers survive—and they do survive—because they create for themselves another persona. They develop a new view of self as an American, relating to a new history, evolving a political position within the new context, finding their way economically and professionally. The old persona (abandoned at age 5 or 12 or 16) remains part of the complex change that must evolve before the new persona can emerge.

There is no way to keep the old self intact when migrating to a new land. The process of conversion—part acculturation, part maturation—begins in the school these children join upon arrival. Dreams of youth, fashioned in another culture and another time, must be both abandoned and rebuilt as the new American persona emerges. Note that this is happening in a particular psychological context created by the "involuntary" status of most immigrants of school age—that is, they did not come of their own free will, but are brought along by parents or other relatives.

The young newcomer does not know why he or she is here. The school is the social institution where the first steps in articulating a new view of self are taken, and it plays a major role in defining that self. The school "tells" the newcomer how he or she is perceived by the host society, mainly through its hidden curriculum, which begins during matriculation and continues through graduation. This image of the newcomer's self that the school reflects is imprinted on the newcomer forever.

As this excellent book by Robert Dentler and Anne Hafner unfolds, we see portraits of schools and districts, some that are ready to accept these children as their own and others that are not. Some present a warm and understanding face, doing things that are positive and effective; in this book they are identified, and their methods are clearly evident. In other school systems, also identified and described in this book, we see an unwillingness to accept these children: These schools are ineffective at teaching them, and for this we will be paying social costs for many years to come.

Dentler and Hafner examine the clear but differing responses that schools and school systems give to the most pressing questions of newcomers: Why am I here? Where do I fit in? What kind of an American can I be? In that process, the authors successfully meet the challenge of helping policymakers and school administrators understand how school districts can respond effectively to the increasing need to educate both immigrant and native-born children who do not speak English. Dentler and Hafner's careful study, pointing the way toward the adoption of some practices and the rejection of others, will bring to educators a firm and learned grounding for the decisions they must make.

This is also a very accessible book. There is no need to know statistics to read, understand, and benefit from its wisdom. Every finding is explained and explored, and the message of the book never gets blurred with researcher's jargon or the mere demonstration of quantitative expertise.

Dentler and Hafner provide what we need from scholars and researchers in order for our society to develop new ways of dealing with old problems. Theirs is the rational argument, yet our history of educating newcomers is not filled with reason; it is governed by politics. This book identifies the correct organizational decisions that must be made in order for a school and district to be effective in meeting the challenge of educating newcomers. But these decisions can only be made in a policy climate that takes the needs of the newcomers seriously and views all their languages as potential bridges to other cultures, other science and art, other philosophy and life experience—bridges our policy should seek to strengthen and expand. In a political climate that champions "English Only" and seeks to deny even emergency medical care to undocumented newcomers and their American-born children, it becomes especially important to recognize what we lose as individuals and what we risk as a nation when we let such short-sighted (and often mean-spirited) visions guide our future.

In education, less is never more. Monolingualism is a hard-won learned condition foisted upon a person who starts life as a potential bilingual. Research points to these subtractive practices as factors in the under-achievement of newcomers. But beyond the narrow view of learning effectiveness or the wider view of structuring opportunities to learn, a policy to make more monolinguals out of potential bilinguals must clearly be seen by all as a policy of diminishing returns.

On behalf of the millions of newcomers in our schools today and those who will grace our shores in the decades ahead, I extend gratitude to Dentler and Hafner. They have written a book that articulates in abundance what must be done in order to succeed at making of newcomers what they each want to be—fully participating citizens.

José R. Llanes
University of Texas–Pan American

# Preface

The study described in this book was designed originally by Robert A. Dentler as part of the work plan filed by the Southwest Regional Laboratory (SWRL) for its subcontract with the Far West Laboratory (FWL). The core of SWRL's work plan was a proposal to create a Metropolitan Center whose staff would focus systematically on the challenges facing educators in metropolitan area districts within the service region comprising California, Arizona, and Nevada. Planning services, demonstrations, development projects, and technical assistance were to be based upon regionally pertinent, knowledge-based models whose dissemination to participating districts would stimulate and guide efforts to improve the educational services of school districts. The metropolitan (or metro) focus stemmed from a conviction that urban, edge city, large suburban, and other districts within metropolitan areas would account for far and away the largest proportion of students in greatest need of improved services. Other agencies were focused at that time on rural schools and students, and it is a fact that the high growth in enrollments in these states between 1980 and 1990 was primarily due to the in-migration of ethnic and language minority children, whose families settled in the metropolitan areas.

The rationale for focusing the study on metro areas in three Far Western states was dual. On one side, it stemmed from the mission of SWRL, which was founded under federal sponsorship in 1965 to assist in educational improvement in these states. On the other side, it grew out of our awareness that the scale of metro area enrollments in California, and the scale of their inclusion of ethnic and language minorities, exceeded all other states save for Hawaii. Elementary and secondary enrollments in California in 1986, for instance, were nearly two times greater than those in New York, the next largest state, and they had been increasing for many years. Only California, Alaska, and Florida public schools increased their enrollments by more than 10% between 1987 and 1992, for example. Minority enrollments in California made up roughly 46% of all students in 1986 and grew to 55% by 1991. Only the enrollments in the District of Columbia, Hawaii, Mississippi, and New Mexico were proportionately higher in shares of minority students in either 1986 or 1991, and each of these systems hosted a large number of either African Americans or Hispanics, whereas California's shares were much more diverse (Snyder & Hoffman, 1993). Arizona's and Nevada's metro districts were included because they were part of the SWRL mission and because they offered the prospect for comparative analysis.

The practical feature of the project grew from consideration of the question of how staff in the SWRL Metro Center might best assist public school administrators to develop programs that served disadvantaged minority students most effectively. At a practical level, project leaders wanted to take a district approach rather than a school-by-school or student-centered approach because school-by-school efforts are too piecemeal and tend not to take root in the neediest or most impacted schools within districts. District strategies have not been closely examined in recent years.

The study was made possible by the willingness of the superintendents and principals in the sample districts to open their offices, records, and schools to our field research. We were treated well by these cordial administrators, school board members, parents, civic officials, teachers, and support staff, and we would like to thank them for their cooperation.

We would also like to acknowledge the work of the following SWRL staff members on this project: Ronald Corwin, Naida Tushnet, Younghee Jang, Marcella Dianda, Jerry Bailey, Cristina Bodinger de Uriarte, Diane Manuel, Anne Baba, Colleen Montoya, David van Broekhuisen, Cristi Carson, David Ditman, Marisela Sifuentes, and Lauren Delgadillo. Drafts of parts of the chapters were written by Ron Corwin, Younghee Jang, Jerry Bailey, and Marcella Dianda.

The mistakes and misinterpretations in this book belong to us alone, of course, but we owe much of the best of it to the guidance and encouragement received from Teachers College Press Series Editor Gary Natriello and Acquisitions Editor Susan Liddicoat. Finally, our thanks to a good and wise educational leader, Herman Moya, retired Superintendent of the Isaac School District, Maricopa County, Arizona.

# 1

# The Challenge of Newcomers

In the 1980s, our country saw the greatest rise in immigration since the beginning of the century. Immigrants currently arrive in the United States at a rate of over one million a year, mostly from Mexico, Central America, and Asia. Because of this unprecedented rise, school districts all over America are grappling with various problems related to their newcomer student populations. Policy analysts, state and local officials, and school administrators all want to know: *What works with newcomers? How do we best meet their special educational needs, including social, health, academic, and language needs?* A central challenge here is the accelerating pace of cultural and socioeconomic diversity of conditions among immigrant children and their families.

The purpose of this book is to describe metropolitan school districts that are successfully meeting the challenge of educating vast numbers of newcomer students. It identifies political, cultural, organizational, programmatic, staff, and instructional features that are associated with higher student achievement and other outcomes. In addition, it examines quantitatively and qualitatively the key differences between districts with comparatively low achievement score gains and those with comparatively high gains.

*Hosting Newcomers* reports on the results of a comparative study of 11 elementary public school districts and 40 of their schools in the metro areas of Arizona, California, and Nevada. The metro areas of the Pacific Southwest received, housed, and educated greater numbers of poor ethnic and language minority students during the 1980s than did all of the other regions of the United States combined. The districts were selected because they showed exceptional enrollment increases from 1980 to 1990, especially in rising numbers of newly arriving children from low-income, immigrant families. Three districts we called high performing, as they showed positive gains in achievement test scores. Five were low performing, and three were stable, showing little change.

We aimed to identify conceptual models of excellent district practices in the treatment of students—models grounded in the experiences and work of educators in enrollment-impacted metro districts—hoping that these models would offer a basis for the exchange of ideas and technical assistance. We asked ourselves, Are there communities, school boards, superintendents, and teachers in the metro areas of the Far West who are doing very well in hosting their newcomers, as well as their longer term students, in spite of the odds stacked against them? Are there districts within rapidly changing communities where achievement scores rise in the very midst of rising social and economic hardships? Perhaps some communities succeed by increased efforts within traditional programs, whereas others adopt new programs and innovate to meet their intensifying challenges. The details of teaching and of service delivery would, we hypothesized, include features that could be extracted to share with other metro districts.

Metro districts where achievement outcomes suggested a marked failure to host newcomers effectively were not of interest in themselves. We did not intend to research patterns of failure or suboptimal educational service, both of which are commonplace and expected under conditions of high enrollments of disadvantaged children. But it would make little sense to describe districts that are succeeding when they have not been contrasted systematically with comparable districts operating under the same regional and demographic environments. Our research therefore scanned a universe of metro districts and sampled from within them those in which socioeconomic conditions were measurably similar yet in which achievement test score changes were higher or lower than the universe average.

## DISADVANTAGED NEWCOMERS

Schooling within a capitalist society is necessarily competitive. Being schooled in America has often meant being graded and sifted until, as a student matures in age, he or she can be classified and treated as an educational winner or loser. This institutional tradition could not only maintain the appearance of contributing to the identification of winners; it could also function both cheaply and ineffectively and still earn public confidence and fiscal support.

Public schools were originally organized to serve the middle classes and the deserving poor from a small number of ethnic groups whose members regarded themselves as the "real Americans." As the first waves of immigrants from other countries reached the nation's shores at the turn of the 19th century,

> The legend has it, that once upon a time the public school was an effective antipoverty agency, that took poor immigrant children and taught them so well that eventually they became affluent Americans. The reality, as Colin Greer shows . . . was quite different: the public schools of the late nineteenth and early twentieth centuries did not help poor children, but instead, failed them in large numbers and forced them out of school. Indeed, the actual function of the public school was just the reverse of the legendary function; it certified the children of the poor as socially inferior at an early age, and thus initiated the process that made many of them economically inferior in adulthood and kept them poor. (Gans, 1972, p. vii)

After this first wave of immigration, ethnic and language minority newcomers were, for the most part, expected to assimilate, to become members of the "real America," or to emulate the ways of those members as best they could. Extremely high proportions of the children of immigrants as well as children of African Americans and Mexicans were among those who did not assimilate and emulate and thus became deeply disadvantaged as competing students. Among those denied equal opportunities to learn at every turn were the grandchildren and great-grandchildren of Africans who entered America as part of a slave caste and Mexicans who found themselves separated from their country as the states of Arizona, California, Texas, and New Mexico were placed under United States rule or who entered later as unwelcome immigrants.

American educational researchers often group certain students under the term *educationally disadvantaged*. Such a student is one "who has been exposed to insufficient educational experiences in at least one of . . . three domains—formal schooling itself, the family, or the community" (Natriello, McDill, & Pallas, 1990, p. 13). These researchers combine five status variables to create the construct of a disadvantageous socioeconomic condition for children who carry these attributes with them into the schoolhouse and the classroom. In descending order of effect, they identify the following as major predispositive factors: (1) racial or ethnic minority status, (2) household poverty, (3) single-parent households, (4) mothers with low educational attainment, and (5) no English proficiency (NEP) or limited English proficiency (LEP). Natriello et al. do not mean that all children with from one to five of these attributes are categorically or uniformly disadvantaged, of course. There are many exceptions to each attribute's effects. Nor are these attributes exhaustive, as others could be substituted or added to the set.

Some educators prefer the term *at-risk* students. Montgomery and Rossi (1994) observe:

Many young people today are becoming at risk of failure in America's schools for the same reason their parents and grandparents became at risk: limited educational opportunities and incentives. And some young people are also becoming at risk due to age-old problems beyond school walls: poor nutrition, inadequate health care, dangerous neighborhoods, abuse, and neglect. . . . In this conceptualization, "risk factors" are variables that decrease the probability that a student will possess the ability, willingness, or opportunities for academic engagement and intellectual development. (pp. 3, 13)

*Disadvantaged* and *at risk* refer to the same sociological categories of children and to the attributes and institutional factors affecting their chances of school learning. But Natriello et al. (1990) warn that the term *at risk* is drawn from public health and criminology and usually refers to groups of individuals who have a markedly higher likelihood of contracting a disease or of committing a felony. They worry that this concept could reinforce the tendency of some policy makers to label poor and minority children in a derogatory way. When the concept of *at risk* is applied in school or classroom practice, it may imply, misleadingly, that predicting outcomes at the individual level is possible.

Both terms—*disadvantaged* and *at risk*—are used in this book, but as our title page suggests, we prefer the term *newcomer* because it refers to the main research concern of this study. As Chapter 2 describes in detail, we selected school districts precisely because they had received exceptionally large numbers of newly arriving children in the 1980s who were from ethnic and language minority, low-income households. The overlap between the underlying subgroups of metro region students in the three states is great: The newcomers to the districts we studied meet the criteria of Natriello et al. (1990) and Montgomery and Rossi (1994) for disadvantagement. A very high proportion of them, in fact, were deemed at risk by the staff we interviewed within the districts.

If we take just one of the status variables—namely, poverty—the magnitude of the problem in the Far Western states becomes apparent. California schools enrolled 651,039 children from impoverished households in 1980 and 897,104 in 1990, an increase of 37.8%. Arizona schools enrolled 90,072 poor children in 1980 and 136,626 in 1990, an increase of 51.7%. Nevada schools enrolled 14,653 poor children in 1980 and 23,065 in 1990, an increase of 57.4% (General Accounting Office [GAO], 1995). The absolute growth in numbers of poor schoolchildren in the three states accounted for 58.8% of the growth in numbers for all 50 states of the United States in the same decade.

Roughly one in every five schoolchildren in these three Far Western states was from a household that fell below the federal poverty line in 1990, and more than 80% of these children lived within metropolitan areas.

Although concentrations of children in poverty were smaller than those in such states as Louisiana, Mississippi, and West Virginia, the concentrations in the latter states were quite uniformly divided between poor Whites and poor African Americans. The concentrations in the Far Western states were vastly more diverse. In addition, concentrations in the Southern states grew at much lower rates during the 1980s.

Very great numbers of poor schoolchildren came to the doors of the metro public schools in the three Far Western states during this decade. The numbers of African American students remained fairly constant over these years, whereas the numbers of Hispanic and Asian and Pacific Island children grew tremendously. The combined impact of tens of thousands of newcomers upon services for NEP and LEP pupils, pupils with special needs, and children with predictably low levels of achievement in literacy and numeracy precipitated a crisis that coincided with a funding crisis in Arizona and California. Arizona increased its per pupil expenditures by only 14%, and California, by only 10% over the decade, for example, while many other states increased by two and three times these percentages (GAO, 1995). Some relatively poor states changed as follows: Arkansas, 41%; Georgia, 47%; and Kentucky, 55%. Wealthy states ranged from a 58% increase in Connecticut to 63% in New Jersey and 47% in Ohio.

As new groups have continued to enter the country, educational policy makers have tended to cluster the newcomers together with the more settled ethnic minorities. In human terms, about one third of all of California's Hispanic and Black students drop out before completing high school. Both Hispanic and Navajo students in Arizona perform on average 2 standard deviations below the average for Anglos on standardized achievement tests. This means that much higher relative proportions of children in poverty live in the metro areas. Finally, it means that both new and older ethnic minority groups in California now share conditions of racial segregation and school failure on a massive scale (see Rumberger & Wilms, 1992). Catterall's (1987) analysis shows how this combination can generate staggering economic and social cost in the form of higher unemployment, lower earnings, higher crime, and greater impacts on human service resources.

## THE QUESTIONS

The characteristics that disadvantaged children bring with them through the schoolhouse door make up the independent background variables of this study. Although they are of inordinate importance, they have been researched extensively since 1960 and therefore are not the phenomena we seek to explain.

We focused on this major question:

- Are there school districts in the metropolitan areas of California, Arizona, and Nevada whose staffs receive, host, and treat their newcomer students so well that they flourish academically, despite challenges that overwhelm other districts?

Such schools, if they exist, we reasoned, must be doing something beneficial for these students. They have somehow found effective ways to teach socioeconomically and linguistically disadvantaged learners.

In addressing this question, we have assumed that (a) the sources of disadvantagement are multiple and include the school environment itself, and (b) schools can, under certain cultural, organizational, and programmatic conditions, partially countervail the negative effects from other sources upon the cognitive development of schoolchildren. If these twin assumptions are valid, then the staggering costs of school failure can be reduced in many communities and perhaps across whole regions, as a result of positive changes of a systemic sort. The alternative is that those costs will escalate very substantially as the numbers of newcomers rise and children of the White middle class become a small subpopulation in the midst of whole school systems that were historically designed and established to serve them.

We also wanted to discover what was distinctive and exceptional about these places as school districts and as communities. So we also asked these questions:

- Do successful districts have distinctive features that form a kind of pattern that contrasts clearly with less successful districts?
- Can we devise a kind of ideal type of what works well academically in hosting low-income ethnic and language minority learners?
- Can the ideal type be transferred feasibly into other interested districts? Or, more likely, are there several overlapping types, rather than one, that fit different situations?

The last question refers to the existence of substantial and obvious differences between very large urban and small edge-city districts and the fact that some schools have predominant concentrations of native Spanish-speaking students while other schools may host 10 or more different language groups. Therefore, we were prepared for the likelihood that one ideal type might not fit all situations. We also recognized that some ideal features are contingent on unique community historical or cultural conditions that cannot be imitated elsewhere.

We focus steadfastly here on several Western metropolitan area schools and districts where the arrival of great numbers of disadvantaged immigrant students since 1980 has had enormous impact. We concentrate on how these districts adjusted and responded to that challenge, subjecting their policies and practices to the keenest scrutiny, and we believe that our findings can be extended to similar highly impacted districts in other areas of the country.

## GUIDING CONCEPTS

A functionalist perspective guided our search, both for successful school districts and for the practices within them that countervail disadvantagement. From this conceptual perspective, opportunities to learn, educational resources, curriculum and instruction, ancillary services, and achievement outcomes are all stratified by the social structural factors of race, ethnicity, language group, family composition, and income.

### Opportunity to Learn

As the U.S. Commissioner of Education James E. Allen (1969) noted more than two decades ago,

> Opportunity for learning means, to me, a community where fathers are employed and where children can learn through their fathers about the dignity of man. It means a community where the population of rats does not exceed the population of children, and where children can learn the values of a healthy society. It means a community of clean streets, of playgrounds, of uncrowded homes, where children can learn the value of living in a free country and the importance of keeping it free. And finally, it means a community free of fear, where children can learn to love life and their fellow man. (p. 81)

Allen's (1969) vision was as large as the economic environment and the community surrounding schoolchildren. Today, by contrast, the term *opportunity to learn* centers more narrowly on the extent to which school districts and schools maintain consistent and reasonably high standards for the delivery of instruction and related services to children and youth. Opportunity to learn today is conceptually keyed to the specific question of whether districts are capable of meeting the learning needs of their learners and whether all children have equal access to quality education.

Stevens (1993) reviewed and summarized the current literature that defines the concept of opportunity to learn. She notes that "the powerful concept of opportunity to learn has been used principally to explain differences among students in comparative international studies of educational achievement and in some small-scale national research studies" (p. 10). Among the four dimensions Stevens identifies is quality of instructional delivery. Brophy and Good (1986) define this feature as the extent to which teachers use teaching practices—that is, coherent lessons—to increase students' academic achievement, whether they use varied pedagogies to meet the needs of all students, and whether they have cognitive command of the subject matter.

Whereas other features of the concept refer principally to matters of curricular content coverage, exposure, and emphasis, including consistency of alignment between what is taught and what is measured in achievement tests, the delivery feature centers upon equity aspects in the quality of instruction.

## Social Structural Dominance

We cannot afford to lose sight of the environment because, other things being equal, public schools and the districts operating them tend to function in ways that maintain the social class and ethnic stratification features of their host communities, states, and the larger regional economy. The learning opportunities they provide are therefore stratified on income, occupational, educational, and housing characteristics of the community's population relative to surrounding communities.

Sociologist Jiobu (1988, 1990) has demonstrated empirically that people in California are highly stratified on the variables of income, occupation, educational attainment, and inclusion in the community and economic life. Furthermore, the strata are systematically correlated with ethnicity, with differing effects on each ethnic group.

However, there is a national cultural norm that acts as a constraint on this structural feature within public schools. The lower the grade level of a group of students, the more concern teachers and administrators express about being fair and unbiased (Garcia, 1992). This is not only a social norm in the teaching and learning environment; it is also an economic norm in a competitive society where, if a contest of skills and work-force productivity is to prevail, talent must have an early chance to show itself in individuals. The culture of many public schools—in contrast to the exceptions, which are the schools that interest us—therefore constructs a kind of game in which the youngest learners are expected to meet on a "level learning field" and to be rewarded differentially by the extent to which they invest observably in the school-going game.

Most ethnic and language minority students, however, come onto the elementary school learning field comparatively unequipped to play this game. Because of their lack of community and family cultural preparation, as well as their relatively scarce preschool learning opportunities, they often cannot meet initial expectations. Their performances, and evaluations of their performances, therefore decline as they continue. Many of these students are thus left out of the circle of social support provided by the larger, Anglo-dominated community. Nor are their families situated politically to secure the help of school staff to advocate for and facilitate their school progress (Bloch & Swadener, 1992).

Their position at the bottom of their local community social system and their concentration in relatively poor communities tend to ensure that their poverty, family vulnerabilities, and language differences will translate over time within school into educational disadvantage. Synthesizing this perspective, Persell (1977) calls it the "process effect of structural dominance" (p. 32).

It is a ubiquitous process. Persell (1977) shows how, in the absence of deliberate efforts to offset structural dominance, nearly all forces within a local public educational system work together to translate high socioeconomic status into high educational achievement. In a competitive environment, arrangements and resources aimed at meeting the needs of low socioeconomic status groups become sacrificed. Such a system takes time to evolve. Its intensity and pervasiveness are shaped locally by history and by state as well as local political cultures.

Some features of structural dominance may change as the economy and the polity change. For example, students from poor families in Elmtown (Hollingshead, 1949) in pre-1950 rural Illinois generally ended their schooling after eighth grade, while Elmtown's upper- and middle-income youth went on to high school and college. In 1940 one in three of Elmtown's youth went to high school for more than a year. Hollingshead found in revisiting Elmtown that, by 1972, eight in ten went on into 12th grade (Hollingshead, 1975). But the point is that today's dropouts still come up out of Elmtown's lowest income strata, even though there are fewer of them because the local economy has changed from needing hired farmhands to needing literate service-industry workers.

Structural dominance is a product of mainstream social and political forces. It applies to groups that subscribe to the mainstream culture. However, children from some subcultures are not part of the American sociopolitical mainstream, and therefore our theory must be enlarged to extend to subcultural minorities, especially a unique category that has castelike qualities. Educational philosopher Howe (1992) has noted, for instance, that

> The . . . ideal . . . of equal educational opportunity supplies the answer to the question of what educational opportunities are indeed worth wanting and thus what educational opportunities are to be equalized among school children. It only makes sense to invite people to participate in schooling (or for people to accept that invitation) if they will be treated as equals. And that is incompatible with defining people in terms of roles they did not shape or endorse. (p. 463)

The point to be emphasized here is that, unlike many prior generations of immigrant groups from northern and southern Europe, which quickly assimilated into the dominant culture, some groups do not wish to, or cannot, invest in the search for an equal opportunity to learn in conventionally mainstream ways. As Howe (1992) observes,

> Caste-like minorities include groups like African Americans and Mexican Americans. Unlike autonomous minorities such as the Amish, they participate significantly in (and are subjugated by) the dominant political-economic community; unlike immigrant minorities such as the American Chinese, they become a part of the political-economic community involuntarily. Because of their peculiar circumstances, rather than adopting the separatist strategies of the Amish or the alternation strategy of the American Chinese, caste-like minorities have adopted an oppositional strategy to preserve their cultural identity. Such a strategy typically entails poor school performance because what is involved in doing well in school requires accepting the values of the dominant culture to which caste-like minorities are in opposition. (p. 467)

The concept of structural dominance does not capture the situation of castelike minorities. Moreover, it does not account, in a postmodern era of tremendously swift changes, for events that sometimes trigger countervailing forces. The theory must be expanded to allow for the possibility that some school districts will make deliberate efforts to help newcomers overcome the grasp of structural dominance. Specifically, we assume that some metropolitan school districts of the West, in their current flux and in the course of receiving great numbers of newcomers, will include some that are struggling intentionally in many ways to countervail the persisting effects of structural dominance.

Structural dominance, in our view, goes a very long way toward explaining the key source of the nation's extreme variations between both inputs and outcomes in American public schooling. Schools evolved first as institutions to socialize the young toward piety and literacy, and second as arrangements through which resources would be concentrated differentially upon the most advantaged socioeconomic and ethnic groups in the society. As credentialing and skill training alike became more critical as determinants of life chances, however, structural dominance came under increasing strain. It has been challenged through every channel of government and at every level as an unfair constraint on racial, gender, class, and other kinds of group equity.

## INTERVENING FACTORS

With individual exceptions, then, a school district's treatment of socioeconomically disadvantaged and language minority students has measurable and forecastable consequences: As the numbers of those students rise, the reading and mathematics achievement test score averages will generally decline.

Among the small subset of districts where this association does not hold—that is, in the deviant cases where achievement scores were much higher than expected—we focused on a few kinds of evidence that we thought might best explain the reasons for the departure from the general trend. They include political culture, expenditures, organization, instructional and educational programs, the informal environment, and health and human services.

### Political Cultures

We define culture as "socially shared cognitive codes and maps, norms of appropriate behavior, assumptions about values and world view, and lifestyle in general" (Delgado-Gaitan & Trueba, 1991, p. 17). Culture in this sense is as applicable to a political entity such as a state or a local school district, or to a school, as it is to villages and tribes. As human service agencies are formed on cultural premises, these organizations embody and are guided by collectively cognitive maps toward what is most valued and toward who should get what resources within their structures.

State political cultures, moreover, vary greatly in how active or passive their agencies are in responding to educational needs among a host of competing service agency activities (Dentler, 1984). Communities within states may correspond with state cultures in important respects, but they also differ in many local historical particulars. A community has localized views about its importance—its self-estimated ability to solve its problems, for instance—and about its stability and longevity. Its adults have shared ideas about whether their children and grandchildren will live out their lives nearby or will move away in order to find jobs and maintain families of their own.

Communities also develop norms about the tolerable scope of ethnic pluralism, allowable subcultural diversity and autonomy, and intergroup or cross-group power sharing. Communities, too, differ substantially in the value priority they assign to the wellness and optimal growth of children. In these and in many other ways, including the possibility in some Western regional communities that the settlement itself is so new as to lack distinctive local features, community culture constitutes a significant source of influence on educational disadvantagement.

## Expenditures

State public education systems vary greatly in their levels of fiscal investment. The variation is affected substantially by differences in per capita wealth from state to state, to be sure, but it also converges on a state's historical and political disposition to invest. Financial researchers refer to this as effort as distinguished from capacity.

Although in the past California was one of the heaviest spenders on public schooling in the West, both as a function of relative wealth and of political will to invest. The communities of California vary greatly in their public school investments. Espinosa and Ochoa (1992) report, for example, that contrary to California law, per pupil expenditures and several expenditure subcategories varied greatly in each year from 1984 through 1989. Specifically, public schools enrolling more than half of their students from African American and Latino households were being short-changed in districts from all over the state. In their intensive analysis of similar data on the Los Angeles Unified School District (LAUSD) for 1984–1985, Espinosa and Ochoa found

> a clear profile of inequality of fiscal structural resources. . . . Allocation of facilities, school capacity, air conditioning, restrooms, school size, classroom size, portable versus permanent classrooms, playground space, site maintenance, library books—all educational resources . . . varied significantly and substantially between schools according to their size and ethnic concentration, with the disparities overwhelmingly favoring white majority schools at the expense of Latino, Afro American and Asian-American majority schools. (p. 96)

Their data on Los Angeles also showed that

> ethnically, linguistically diverse schools were significantly enrolled over capacity, were overcrowded, were on year round schedules and had inadequate

facilities and teachers who were less experienced and were more likely to be substitutes than was true in white majority schools. (p. 96)

Therefore, our concern with political culture and communities includes financial investment differences among the sampled districts.

## The Organization of School Districts and Schools

The structure of a complex, formal public service organization like a school district may have evolved gradually in response to structural dominance or the ideals of the funding community. Or it may have been changed intentionally in order to meet changing demographic, economic, or political trends. A school district seeking to comply with a court order to desegregate, for example, must necessarily be changed to provide for new staffing and student assignments.

Thus local policy makers and educators may have consciously restructured their district, or at least some of their schools and programs, since 1980 in order to better host and respond to rising numbers of disadvantaged newcomers. Alternatively, changes in organization may have taken place more spontaneously and apart from deliberate policy planning. This is part of what we wanted to search out. Wills and Peterson (1992) researched ways in which state reform legislation and mandates, regarded generally as the major source of school change during the 1980s, are accelerated or impeded, and complied with or modified, by local superintendents and their responses to conditions in their local environments. Their study supports other evidence (Cuban, 1984; Firestone, 1989) showing that local district and individual school responses and reactions to reform imperatives are of critical intervening importance. Other studies of local school programs (Wehlage, Rutter, & Smith, 1989) show how programs can be designed to intervene effectively between the "risks" disadvantaged learners carry with them and the likelihood that they will flourish academically and remain in school.

## The Design and Delivery of Instruction and Educational Programs

In the quest for schools that have done well, researchers sometimes seek out districts claiming to have adopted new educational or social service programs. This makes eminent sense, as federal and state agencies compete perennially to name, formulate, and fund programs that are intended to improve conditions for the disadvantaged. All three levels of government tend to operate programmatically; thus a school with a well-funded Spanish bilingual program operating in response to, say, a three-fold increase in NEP and LEP students has obviously acted to create a programmatic way to host its newcomers.

A recent review of research into such practices inventoried the most successful instructional practices currently in use with NEP and LEP students (Garcia, 1992). We have used this inventory in comparing our sample of districts. In addition, we have made use of the conclusions reached by Nel (1992) and Hernandez (1992) in their recent reviews of good multicultural instructional methods for use with disadvantaged learners. From the standpoint of educational practice in general, improvements in instruction and programs are the very core of responsive adaptation to the increasingly imperative needs of disadvantaged children (Slavin, Karweit, & Madden, 1989).

## The Informal Environment

Yet, what may be truly countervailing the conventionally indifferent treatment of disadvantaged students might not have received a program label or resource budget. It could be homemade. It might lack explicit goal statements or written plans and still be powerfully effective. Moreover, what staff and community volunteers actually do in interacting with students each day, whether implicit and even partially incomplete in its intentions as opposed to preplanned, determines the impact of the school organization upon otherwise vulnerable students.

Political culture, expenditures, school organization, and educational programs matter tremendously, then, but they are probably far less enduringly influential than are the characteristics of the informal interpersonal environment within schools and classrooms and on playgrounds. Even programs such as cooperative learning, which are designed to improve that environment, depend for their ultimate efficacy on the implicit qualities of social interaction—the sentiments of regard and interest and hope, for instance, and the norms of dignity and social respect. We may not have labels for them; yet such behaviors can be witnessed by any trained observer. We have studied who teaches what in the sampled districts and have appraised differences in the quality of interaction with some care.

## Health and Human Services

For all children and youth, but most crucially for the disadvantaged, the scope and quality of services—social, protective, health, psychological, and other—are as pertinent today as are the organization and delivery of academic instruction. Therefore, we have included a multiple-case comparison of the districts on this dimension.

Our sampled districts, and the metropolitan area universe from which they were drawn, are localities that were very heavily impacted by adverse health and crime trends during the 1980s. State profiles contained in the *Kids Count Data Book* (Center for the Study of Social Policy, 1992) show that trends in children in poverty, percentage of children living in single-parent families, percentage of all births that are to single teens, and other indicators of service needs worsened between 1980 and 1990 in Arizona, California, and Nevada. Social and health services linked closely with schools or operated from within school districts are often the first line of defense or defeat for newly arriving families in poverty.

## PREVIEW OF THE BOOK

We agree with Natriello et al. (1990) "that successfully educating the population of disadvantaged children will demand a monumental increase in the level of resources that this country devotes to this task" (p. 13). Without greatly improved funding, there is little likelihood of reversing the multiplier effects of increasing disadvantaged status. If and when the resources become available, however, we want to make sure we know what to give the highest developmental priority.

The disadvantaged status of student newcomers in the history of conventional public schools in the United States is, in our view, a history of failing to provide opportunities to learn successfully for precisely those who arrive at school least equipped to compete academically by virtue of low economic and divergent cultural resources in their families. We have gone in search of districts that have worked hard to countervail this tradition and to provide fitting and even excellent opportunities to learn to minority newcomers.

The factors identified in this chapter will guide discussions throughout the remainder of this book. Chapter 2 summarizes the research design and the methods and instruments used in the project. Chapter 3 reviews differences in educational and instructional quality between low- and high-achieving districts and integrates data on differences in teaching staffs. Chapter 4 examines the history, local cultures, and community and resource features of the sampled districts. Chapter 5 examines the organization of the districts and their schools. Chapter 6 compares the social, health, and other service program features. Chapter 7 synthesizes our findings and interprets them for their contributions to models of district and school success.

The goal that inspired this field study—that of giving technical assistance to metro area school districts and schools in Arizona, California, and Nevada based on models of effectiveness in hosting newcomers—was never fulfilled. Arizona and California entered a severe economic depression in 1992. Although Nevada exceeded the national average in ability to raise education revenue in that year, the other two states fell well below that average and thus into a class with such historically poor states as Alabama, Arkansas, Idaho, and Mississippi (GAO, 1995). In addition, the operating agenda of SWRL changed substantially during the period of the field study and the goal of giving technical assistance was dropped in favor of other objectives.

We have co-authored this book based on the project in the conviction that its findings will contribute to the applied sociology of education and to the quest of practitioners for ways to redesign and strengthen school districts. We owe this to the educators in the school districts we studied and to the larger public whose resources supported this inquiry.

This book's contribution rests in identifying some of the practices that matter most for educators, community leaders, and others who are committed to improving conditions that shape the opportunities of disadvantaged newcomers. The book can aid local officials and administrators in making changes in their organization and educational programs that can benefit their newcomer children.

# 2
# The Shape of the Study

To answer the study's research questions, we wanted to look at newcomer immigrant students in a sample of school districts that was reflective of the broad range of districts in which these children reside. However, our mandate at the regional lab was to serve the nation's Western region; thus the sample was limited to California, Nevada, and Arizona. As pointed out in Chapter 1, a comparative case study was carried out on 11 public school districts and 40 of their schools in the metropolitan areas of California, Arizona, and Nevada. The districts selected showed exceptional enrollment increases from 1980 to 1990, especially in rising numbers of newly arriving children from minority, low-income, and immigrant families. We examined qualitatively and quantitatively the key differences between districts with low achievement gains over time and those with comparatively high gains over time. This chapter describes in detail the study's sample, instruments, procedures, data collection methods, data analysis methods, and limitations.

## SAMPLE

We used a two-step process to choose a purposive sample of districts. First we identified a pool of potential districts, then selected case study sites from that pool.

### Identifying a Pool of Potential Districts

We began by searching for public school districts within Metropolitan Statistical Areas (MSAs) that had experienced very large demographic changes during the 1980s relative to other districts. We concentrated on identifying districts that between 1980 and 1990 had simultaneously (a) experienced large increases in numbers of low-income students (i.e., from homes officially classified as below the poverty line) or students with limited English proficiency and (b) demonstrated extraordinary positive or negative changes in standardized achievement test scores in reading and math.

The potential universe was defined as approximately 1,100 school districts in California, Arizona, and Nevada. That number was necessarily reduced 37% by excluding rural districts within the MSAs (which were outside the scope of the study). It was also necessary to exclude some districts for which compatible data were unavailable. In addition, because of technical quality considerations, we excluded districts that had enrollments below 2,000 or fewer than 100 students with assessment data for any one grade level.

Next, measures of poverty, language proficiency, and ethnicity were obtained from a variety of sources in addition to the U.S. Census, including the California Basic Education Data System (CBEDS), the California Assessment Program (CAP), Nevada State Department of Education reports, and Arizona State Department of Education reports.

For California and Arizona, each district was assigned a composite index score based on positive change (increase) between 1980 and 1990 in proportional enrollment of minority, LEP, and poor students. The 30 districts in California and 10 districts in Arizona scoring highest on this composite index were then examined in detail. Districts whose total composite score was due to the overwhelming influence of only one factor were excluded from further consideration. Preference was given to districts with high absolute levels of poor and minority students. Also, changes in minority population, language proficiency, and poverty were given priority over changes in population size.

Examination of school districts in Nevada revealed only two MSAs and allied school districts: Clark County (Las Vegas metro area) and Washoe County (Reno metro area). These were the two districts used in the study.

## Selecting Case Study Sites

In our second step, from the larger pool we selected 11 sites that represented a range of improvement/deterioration in test scores. Six districts were chosen in California, three in Arizona, and two in Nevada (because Nevada has only two metropolitan areas). We sorted these into three groups, those with relatively large improvements in test scores over time, those with large declines in test scores, and those with little change in scores.

Two of the sample districts in California and one in Arizona had high positive change scores in achievement. These three we termed "high-performing" districts. Four of the eleven—three in California and one in Arizona—we termed "low-performing" districts. Four of the eleven—two in Nevada, one in Arizona, and one in California—showed little or no change; we termed them "stable performers." Table 2.1 shows the ranking of the 11 districts by standardized test score change over time.

Change in achievement was measured by a standard score, a standardized measure that allowed us to compare districts across tests. A standard score indicates the relative standing of the raw score in a distribution, or how many standard deviations a score falls above or below the mean. A change in achievement standard score provides two important pieces of information. First, the magnitude of the score indicates how many standard deviations the observation falls from the mean. Second, the sign of the standard score indicates whether the score is above (+) or below (–) the mean. Thus, if a standardized change in achievement $z$ score was 1.0, this tells us that the district's gain in achievement over time was 1 standard deviation above the mean.

Cut points for the "stable performer" category were decided upon arbitrarily, but they have a rather obvious logic to them. Four districts exhibiting "little change" had standard scores ranging from –.60 to +.68, between two thirds of a standard deviation below and two thirds of a standard deviation above the average. The three high-performing districts with the highest change in achievement showed score changes ranging from +.74 to 1.44. In other words, they ranged from about three quarters of a standard deviation above the mean to about 1.5 standard deviations above the mean in change. The low-performing "high negative" districts had

**Table 2.1 Achievement Change Over Time, Sample Districts**

| Performance Group | District | Change in Achievement |
|---|---|---|
| HIGH PERFORMERS | Isaac (AZ) | 1.44 |
| (high positive change) | Rosemead (CA) | .80 |
| | National (CA) | .74 |
| | | |
| STABLE PERFORMERS | Franklin McKinley (CA) | .68 |
| (little change) | Washoe County (NV) | .40 |
| | Clark County (NV) | -.30 |
| | Balsz (AZ) | -.60 |
| | | |
| LOW PERFORMERS | San Gabriel (CA) | -1.00 |
| (high negative change) | Fresno (CA) | -1.11 |
| | Sunnyside (AZ) | -1.32 |
| | Mountain View (CA) | -1.43 |

standard score changes ranging from −1.00 to −1.43, scoring from 1 to 1.5 standard deviations below the mean.

We had two primary reasons for sampling an array of districts in this way. First, it is the comparisons among them that permit us to infer whether a factor is present in the high-performing districts and absent in all or most of the others. Second, evidence from the low-performing districts should offer clues to the impediments that slow or obstruct school improvement. Some of these impediments can be reduced by districts determined to upgrade their performance.

## Description of the Districts

As a result of the selection design and procedures described above, 11 public school districts were visited and researched in depth between May and November 1992. Table 2.2 shows a summary of the sample district characteristics as of 1990. Below we describe changes in the selected districts overall between 1980 and 1990, then go on to examine each district in detail. The three Arizona districts are profiled first, followed by the six California districts and the two Nevada districts.

The districts chosen as case study sites differ widely in how the composition of their student body changed and how they responded to these changes. Four districts had large increases in the percentage of minority students and LEP students (San Gabriel, Rosemead, National, and Mountain View). Four were severely impacted by increases in the proportion of minority, LEP, and low-income students (Fresno, Franklin McKinley, Isaac, and Balsz). One (Sunnyside) was impacted by increases in the proportion of minority and low-income students (Corwin, 1994). Washoe County and Clark County had some increases in percentages of minority, LEP, and poor students, but they were not nearly as large as those experienced by districts in other states.

Four of the districts were impacted not only by increases in the proportion of Asian and Hispanic students served but also by accompanying increases in the proportion of LEP students served (San Gabriel, Rosemead, Franklin McKinley, and Fresno). Because of the large variety of different native languages represented in their student population (Spanish, Cantonese, Mandarin, Korean, Vietnamese, Thai, and Hmong), the challenges in these districts were greater than those faced by districts with increases only in the number of Spanish-speaking students (National, Mountain View, Sunnyside, and Isaac).

The districts chosen have very high minority enrollments, with 9 out of the 11 having 50% or greater minority populations. The districts have high enrollments of students in poverty, averaging 37%, and ranging from

**Table 2.2 Study Sample—1990**

| District | Enroll-ment | No. of Schools | % in Poverty | % Minority | % Ethnic Compo-sition[a] | Major Immigrant Groups | % LEP |
|---|---|---|---|---|---|---|---|
| Isaac AZ | 6,20 | 7 | 69 | 79 | 72-H 6-B | Mexican | 33 |
| Rosemead CA | 3,20 | 5 | 16 | 87 | 53-H 30-A 4-O | Mexican, SE Asian, Chinese | 26 |
| National CA | 6,20 | 10 | 29 | 90 | 68-H 6-B 13-A | Mexican, Filipino, Cent. Amer. | 30 |
| Franklin McKinley CA | 9,98 | 13 | 27 | 88 | 53-H 7-B 28-A | Mexican, Chinese, Vietnam | 24 |
| Washoe Co. NV | 40,00 | 52? | 16 | 21 | 11-H 4-A 6-O | Mexican, Filipino | 5 |
| Clark Co. NV | 120,00 | 151 | 21 | 32 | 13-H 14-B 5-O | Mexican, Filipino, Chinese | 5 |
| Balsz AZ | 2,30 | 6 | 63 | 54 | 33-H 12-B | Mexican | 11 |
| San Gabriel CA | 3,50 | 7 | 15 | 75 | 41-H 30-A 4-O | Mexican, Chinese, Vietnamese | 29 |
| Fresno CA | 75,00 | 81 | 39 | 67 | 36-H 10-B 21-A | Mexican, SE Asian, Cent. Amer. | 20 |
| Sunnyside AZ | 13,80 | 15 | 70 | 71 | 65-H 6-B 4-A | Mexican | 13 |
| Mt. View CA | 8,80 | 11 | 29 | 96 | 90-H 1-B 5-A | Mexican, Chinese | 40 |

*Sources:* U.S. Census; CA: CBEDS, district sources; AZ: AZ SDE reports, NV: NV SDE reports

[a] H = Hispanic, B = Black, A = Asian, O = other

15% to 69%. The overall U.S. poverty rate is 21% (Wright, 1996). The districts also have high enrollments of LEP students. LEP enrollment percents range from 5% to 40%, averaging about 21%.

**Arizona.** Balsz is a small school district located within Phoenix and Maricopa County in Arizona. Half of its students are ethnic minorities: 33% Hispanic, 12% African Americans, and 6% Native American and Asian combined. In 1990, 93% of the children younger than 18 years old were citizens, and 13% of children aged 5 to 13 lived in linguistically isolated households, defined as a household in which no one age 14 years or older speaks only English and no other person age 14 or older who speaks another language speaks English very well (U.S. Census Bureau, 1994). The median household income in 1989 was $21,160.

The Isaac School District is also located within Phoenix and Maricopa County in Arizona. Some 79% of those enrolled are ethnic minorities: 72% Hispanic, 6% African American, and 1% other minorities. Isaac is one of the oldest and poorest school districts in Arizona (median household income in 1989 was $17,803). Between 1980 and 1990, its student composition changed from 70% Anglo to about 70% Hispanic. Of the children younger than 18 years old, 89% were citizens, and 18% of children aged 5 to 13 lived in linguistically isolated households in 1990 (U.S. Census Bureau, 1994).

Sunnyside, located in South Tucson in Arizona, enrolls about 13,800 students. Some 65% of the student body are Hispanic, 6% African American, and 4% Asian. In 1990, 95% of children under 18 were citizens, and only 8% of children aged 5 to 13 lived in linguistically isolated households. The median household income in 1989 was $21,748 (U.S. Census Bureau, 1994).

**California.** The Franklin McKinley School District is located in San Jose, one of the largest cities in Northern California. The median household income in 1989 was $25,494. About 90% of its students are ethnic minorities: 53% Hispanic, 28% Asian, and 7% Black. The district experienced a large increase in poor and LEP students from 1980 to 1990. Of children younger than 18, 80% were citizens, and 21% of its children aged 5 to 13 lived in linguistically isolated households in 1990 (U.S. Census Bureau, 1994).

Fresno is one of the largest K–12 districts in California and is located in the Central Valley. Of its students, 36% are Hispanic, 21% are Asian, and 10% are African American. The median household income in 1989 was $24,923. In 1990, 88% of children younger than 18 were citizens, and 20%

of children aged 5 to 13 lived in linguistically isolated households (U.S. Census Bureau, 1994).

The National School District is located in the metro area of San Diego, California, about 10 miles above the Mexican border. About two thirds of its students are Hispanic, 6% Black, and 13% Asian. Almost a third of the district's students are LEP, which represents a 50% increase over the past decade. In 1989, the median household income was $22,129. Of children younger than 18, 85% were citizens in 1990, and 26% of children aged 5 to 13 lived in linguistically isolated households (U.S. Census Bureau, 1994).

The small Rosemead School District is in the west central portion of the San Gabriel Valley, 10 miles east of Los Angeles. Its student population consists of 53% Hispanic, 30% Asian, and 4% other minorities. Rosemead currently hosts students from 18 different language groups. Its median household income in 1989 was $29,770. Only 78% of children younger than 18 were citizens, and fully 35% of children aged 5 to 13 lived in linguistically isolated households in 1990 (U.S. Census Bureau, 1994).

The San Gabriel School District is adjacent to the Rosemead School District in the Los Angeles area. Of its students, 41% are Hispanic, 30% Asian, and 4% other minorities. Its median household income in 1989 was $29,905. Of children younger than 18, 80% were citizens, and 29% of children aged 5 to 13 lived in linguistically isolated households in 1990 (U.S. Census Bureau, 1994).

The Mountain View School District is located in the San Gabriel Valley near the foothills in the Los Angeles basin. Of its students, 90% are Hispanic and 5% are Asian. The median household income in 1989 was $28,034. Of children younger than 18, 80% were citizens, and 35% of children aged 5 to 13 lived in linguistically isolated households in 1990 (U.S. Census Bureau, 1994).

**Nevada.** The Clark County School District, located in the Las Vegas area, enrolls over 120,000 students in its grades K–12, 14% of whom are African American, 13% Hispanic, and 5% other minorities. The county's median household income in 1989 was $30,746. In 1990, 97% of its students were citizens, and 4% of children aged 5 to 13 lived in linguistically isolated households (U.S. Census Bureau, 1994).

The Washoe County School District, in the Reno area, enrolls about 40,000 students in its grades K–12, 11% of whom are Hispanic, 4% Asian, 3% Native American, and 3% other minorities. About 5% of students in Nevada schools are LEP. The county's median household income in 1989 was $31,891. In 1990, 96% of its students were citizens, and 4% of children aged 5 to 13 lived in linguistically isolated households (U.S. Census Bureau, 1994).

## INSTRUMENTATION

The major dependent variable in this study consists of a standardized measure of change in district-level achievement in mathematics and reading between 1984 and 1990, as measured by standardized achievement test scores. Positive change over time in achievement was defined as the "success" measure, mainly because standardized achievement test scores are available and because they are the common currency of educational research and development. However, defining success solely in terms of standardized achievement scores is not desirable, because such measures reflect only part of students' knowledge and skills.

A well-documented relationship exists between demographic variables and achievement. In particular, research evidence from many different sources shows that the greater the number of poor and disadvantaged students, minority and LEP students, the lower the test scores. This pattern supports the structural dominance hypothesis (Persell, 1977).

### Change in Academic Achievement

As we described previously, we sorted the local educational agencies (LEAs) by level of demographic change and identified those with the highest change. Next we selected districts that exhibited the largest positive test score gain and, conversely, the largest decrease in test scores. Because test scores were not widely available for high schools, it was decided to focus primarily on the elementary grades. Therefore, it is important to note that only test scores for grades 3, 6, and 8 were used for all districts (including unified districts). We selected districts with the greatest positive change in achievement, contrasting sites with the greatest negative change, and others that were relatively stable over time. Our original larger pool of chosen districts was reduced for purposes of the site visits. These districts were ranked according to their change in achievement score.

Two caveats should be mentioned pertaining to the process we used to identify districts. First, selections were made based on the *relative change* in achievement. Some of the districts that showed the highest gains over time still had scores that were low in the absolute sense (even though they had improved). Second, positive change in average achievement can be accounted for in several different ways. Even when we focus on relative change over time, it is still difficult to explain reasons for gain or decline over time. When test scores increase, does this indicate better teaching, or is it due to changes in district characteristics? It might be a consequence of change in the percentage of children tested (e.g., change in student mobility rate), or it could be due to different kinds of children who have moved into the area over time (e.g., healthy children). Nevertheless, if certain patterns persist after a number of confounding variables are allowed for, the approach can be illuminating even when changes in test scores do not reflect actual higher achievement.

We looked at the absolute rank of the 11 districts on standardized achievement tests in grades 1–8, for reading and math (see Table 2.3 for districts' absolute rankings). Three large districts (Washoe County, Clark County, and Fresno) all scored above the national average on reading and math and scored at the top of the group (averaging about 54 for reading and 59 for math). There was a significant positive correlation between number of students in a district and reading score ($r = .40$). The correlation between district size and math score was not significant.

Three smaller districts (San Gabriel, Rosemead, and Franklin McKinley) scored above average in math but below the 50th percentile in reading. Two of the districts that showed the largest relative gains over time (National and Isaac) scored near the bottom of the group of districts in absolute rank in both reading and math, around the 30th percentile in read-

**Table 2.3  Absolute Rank on Standardized Achievement Tests, Reading and Math, National Percentiles**

| District | Reading | Math | District |
|---|---|---|---|
| Washoe Co. NV | 55 | 61 | Clark County NV |
| Clark County NV | 55 | 59 | Fresno CA |
| Fresno CA | 50 | 59 | San Gabriel CA |
| San Gabriel CA | 46 | 58 | Rosemead CA |
| Franklin McKinley CA | 38 | 53 | Washoe Co. NV |
| Sunnyside AZ | 38 | 50 | Franklin McK CA |
| Balsz AZ | 38 | 40 | Mt. View CA |
| Rosemead CA | 34 | 38 | Balsz AZ |
| Isaac  AZ | 32 | 38 | National CA |
| National CA | 28 | 35 | Isaac AZ |
| Mt. View CA | 22 | 32 | Sunnyside AZ |

*Sources:* CA, AZ, and NV SDE reports.

ing and the 35th percentile in math nationally. It is important to keep in mind that the focus of the study is on achievement gain, not on absolute ranking. Comparing districts in an absolute sense is unreliable and does not take into account contextual variables.

## Differential Patterns of Achievement

Several variables should be considered when attempting to account for differences in achievement. The first one is district size. The districts in this study vary greatly in size, ranging from Balsz with about 2,300 students to Clark County with about 120,000 students. In general, we expected large districts to be low performers and small districts to be high performers, mainly because of the former's frequent financial problems and their general failure to educate a high proportion of their students (McDonnell & Hill, 1993).

In general, small districts are overrepresented in the high-performer group (all three are under 7,000) and large districts are overrepresented in the low-performer group (three out of four are over 7,000). However, Table 2.2 also shows that very small districts (<5,000) are dispersed throughout all three categories—in the high-positive, little-change, and high-negative groups.

It is worth noting, by contrast, that district size positively predicts reading national percentile rank. However, it is important to point out that large districts in the sample have fewer minority students than small districts ($r = -.54$) and have fewer LEP students ($r = .49$). Implications of the variable of enrollment size are examined in detail in Chapter 5.

Another variable that could be related to student achievement is average district school size. School sizes in sampled districts ranged from 474 to 888. We found that although low performers were more likely to have larger schools, the trend was inconsistent. There did not seem to be more high-performing districts in the top or bottom half of the school-size distribution, and one low-performing district had the smallest average school size.

Another variable that may be related to differential patterns of achievement is the percentage of minorities (specifically, Asians) in a district. As part of our data gathering, we calculated the percentage of students in each ethnic group in each district. The average percentage of Asian students was 12%. Two out of the four high-performing districts had a high percentage of Asian students (Rosemead, 30%, and Franklin McKinley, 28%). However, two other districts (San Gabriel, 30%, and Fresno, 21%) also had similar high percentages of Asian students and were low-performing districts. A look at Table 2.3 shows that no districts with higher than average percentages of Asian students scored above the 50th percentile in reading, whereas three districts with high percentages of Asian students scored above the 50th percentile in math.

The category "Asian" melds together very high-achieving subgroups such as Koreans, Filipinos, and Chinese Americans with low-achieving subgroups such as newly arrived Southeast Asians or Hmong. The possibility should be kept in mind that the percentage of Asian students may be a contributing factor in explaining high positive change in achievement, especially in mathematics.

Another factor that may influence differential patterns of achievement is type of district: elementary (K–6 or K–8) or unified (K–12). Only three districts in the sample were unified. Although only test scores for grades 3, 6, and 8 were used to rank districts, the unified districts were low performers (with the exception of Washoe County, which showed a slight positive change in achievement: +.40). In fact, two of the unified districts were at the bottom of the ranking. By contrast, the top four high-performing districts were K–6 or K–8 and did not include high schools. This is probably related to the fact that unified districts tend to be larger, and larger districts tended to show high negative change.

In addition, some evidence in the literature suggests that the state of the art in pedagogy, support services, and programs for language minority students is more developed at the elementary than at the secondary level in schools (Berman et al., 1992). Thus elementary districts may tend to show higher gains than unified districts because of the more well-developed programs and support services at lower grade levels. In this study, many secondary schools visited lacked adequate models or information about "what works" and relied on traditional instructional programs and models.

Increases in average student achievement may reflect variation or changes in the proportion of students who are tested. Districts vary greatly in the percentage of students who take state achievement tests. Excluding students who are non-English-speaking or who have limited proficiency in English is a common practice. In particular, districts with high proportions of LEP students often do not test as many of these students as do districts with fewer LEP students. In some cases, schools may test some students in math but not in reading (because math is less language-dependent than reading). If the number of such students grows, and the number of students taking the test decreases, change in average achievement may not in fact actually mean that the district is successfully meeting its students' needs.

Correlations show that the higher the percentage of LEP students in a district, the fewer the total number of students tested (correlations range from –.66 for third grade to –.43 for eighth grade). At the third-grade level, this phenomenon may be problematic, at least for some California districts. On average, about 91% of third-grade students were tested in all California districts in 1989–90, but the range tested was .25 to 1.00. In the sampled California districts, 76% of third graders were assessed in 1989–90. However, Mountain View tested only 45% of its third graders and National, only 67%.

One way in which a district could show gains over time would be to decrease the number of limited-English-proficient (and thus low-scoring) students tested. However, correlations for California districts show that, in general, the higher the percentage of children tested in a district, the higher the achievement gains ($r$ = .30 to .40).

An analysis was done of the number of students tested from school years 1984–85 to 1988–89 for California districts only (these data were not available from other districts). Only low-performer Fresno and high-performer Rosemead tested more students over the time interval: up 16% and 6%, respectively. The remainder of districts tested slightly fewer students, from 1% to 5%. Fresno and Rosemead, along with San Gabriel, assessed the highest percentage of LEP students in 1989–90: 87%. Franklin McKinley tested 84%; National, 79%; and Mountain View, 68%. National and Rosemead were identified as high-performing districts. Because Rosemead increased the number of students tested, it should not have shown higher scores. National decreased its percentage tested over time by 5%, and tested only 67% of its third graders in 1989–90; thus its positive gain over time (.74 $z$ score) may be partly due to the effects of testing fewer children.

## Rating Scales

In order to include measures other than student achievement, we developed five rating scales relating to school effectiveness. The school effectiveness literature has shown evidence that school environment, special programs, and teacher and curriculum quality all have an influence on school-level achievement (Lee & Bryk, 1988; O'Day & Smith, 1993). Borrowing from theory and practice, we used items from large-scale national and other survey instruments (e.g., the NELS:88 School and Teacher Questionnaires). Items were also developed on the basis of field experience and from reviewing effective schools research (Castaneda, 1992; Collier, 1992; Cuban, 1984; Means, Chelemer, & Knapp, 1991). Each of the five scales was intended to measure a facet of educational quality. We theorized that these five concepts were important in measuring different factors of school district success and could be estimated by observers at the school site.

The five scales we developed were: the Quality of Education (QE), the Quality of Integration (QI), the Quality of Multiculturalism (QM), the Quality of Organization (QO), and the Quality of Teaching (QT). The scales are reproduced in their entirety in the Appendix. The following descriptions include both the rationale for each scale and some sample item topics:

- The Quality of Education scale was developed because of the necessity of including a general educational quality factor that incorporates a broader sense of high standards, shared community, and a positive environment for learning. QE includes items referring to high standards and expectations, focus on student achievement, faculty involvement and high morale, positive staff-student interactions, a sense of shared community, social environment, use of cross-age and peer tutoring, cooperative learning, and a strong school spirit.
- The Quality of Integration scale, which focuses mainly on multi-ethnic inclusiveness, was used because overall inclusion or integration factors may be related to the overall school climate and to student outcomes. Items measure the racial/ethnic composition of the student body and faculty, tracking and promotion policies regarding ethnic and lingual minority students, degree of racial/ethnic distinctions, and integration of different groups of students socially and in class.
- The Quality of Multiculturalism scale was included to ascertain to what extent ESL and bilingual classes are found in a school and how supportive the school community is for multicultural populations. These factors have bearing on student outcomes, broadly conceived. The scale includes items on whether a school offers ESL or bilingual classes, availability of tutoring in students' native language, use of bilingual teachers or aides, use of bilingual communications, use of translators, use of languages other than English, use of multicultural instructional materials, library holdings in languages other than English, degree of segregation of minority students, diverse student membership in student activities, attitudes on diversity, and staff training in multicultural awareness.
- The Quality of Organization scale was designed to measure structural supports for newcomers, including use of ability grouping, lab facilities, availability of staff community liaisons, and classroom management. Its items focus on use of ability grouping; availability of lab facilities for reading, math, language, and computer learning; provision of in-service training for teachers; use of parent or community liaisons; parent-teacher conferences; PTA; and handling of student misconduct.
- The Quality of Teaching scale was included to measure the strength and quality of classroom instruction. The quality of instruction has been

found to be an important factor in student achievement. The scale includes items on academic press, expectations for homework, focus on academics, use of a variety of teaching strategies, support for in-service education, degree to which teachers coordinate their course content with other teachers, administrative support for new ideas, cooperation among staff members, degree of teacher talk and working together, teachers' expectations of student capability, and availability of broad learning opportunities.

After a day observing and interviewing in a school, each of two field researchers filled out five scales independently. For each item, researchers chose from a 1 = strongly disagree to a 6 = strongly agree. Scores for all items were added up for a scale score. A "good" score would be high on that factor. Afterward, the team matched ratings and reached a joint rating by consensus. This allowed a pooling of observations that compensated for behaviors seen by one researcher but not by the other (Dentler, Baltzell, & Chabotar, 1983).

Reliability of school scales was ascertained in two ways: inter-rater agreement and internal consistency. The overall inter-rater agreement (for all raters) was only moderately high at .74. However, on four of the scales (QE, QI, QM, and QT), 95% to 97% of the raters were within plus or minus one point of each other. Inter-rater agreement on the QO scale was low (.69). We believe that this may be because of the poor quality of the scale.

Three of the scales showed high internal consistency reliability. QE's reliability was .90, QT's reliability was .83, and QM's reliability was .90. Two scales showed only moderate internal consistency (QO at .69 and QI at .76).

## PROCEDURES AND DATA COLLECTION

The approach taken to visiting sites and collecting data was based on procedures for multiple case studies developed and utilized by Dentler et al. (1983), Louis, Kell, and Dentler (1984), and Yin (1986). The approach is grounded on the premise that cases may be made comparable to the extent that they are selected systematically and purposively and are analyzed by a common set of procedures and standards. The multiple case study is ideally suited to a project guided by conceptual concerns with such general variables as community political cultures, organizational structures, and respondent perceptions and expressed attitudes about change and the reception of newcomers.

## Procedures

The group of 12 field researchers who were to visit the sites to collect data was trained for the project in the spring of 1992. The members included SWRL professional staff who were educational researchers, anthropologists, applied linguists, sociologists, and a journalist. The six teams of two people were of mixed gender and diverse racial and ethnic background wherever feasible.

It was intended that each team would visit at least two districts—one with high positive achievement gain scores and one other. As the scheduling of visits became protracted, however, team members were assigned to other SWRL projects and this aim was compromised. In addition, a few people who had not been part of the group training were assigned as site visitors in the fall of 1992.

SWRL representatives wrote and telephoned district superintendents, requesting the opportunity to visit and to include the district in the project. Two superintendents elected not to participate, so alternative districts were chosen. Other superintendents agreed but delayed the visits until the fall of 1992. As superintendents responded and designated liaison coordinators, SWRL outlined the visit plans and indicated the documentary data the two field researchers would need, including persons to interview on site. A district profile sheet was completed, which included the superintendent's name, number, contact persons and numbers, schools to be visited, and demographic information about the district.

## Data Collection

Researchers collected data on a few sites between May and June 1992 and on the remainder between September and November 1992. Of the 12 districts visited, one was not included in the subsequent analysis because the timing of the visit was poor, the two visiting researchers lacked prior project training for this study, and the reception to their visit was unfriendly and uncooperative.

SWRL obtained lists of all the schools within each district, along with their demographic characteristics. We targeted certain schools as representative of high-minority, high-poverty, or high-LEP populations, and recommended to the districts that these schools be visited. In the main, district contacts were agreeable, but in two of the cases superintendents or district contacts specified their own choice of one or more school sites. In general, schools selected and visited were viewed by data collectors as representative.

Data were collected from some high schools and junior high schools. However, most of the project's research effort was concentrated on elementary schools, programs, and personnel because of limitations in the achievement test score data set.

Most site visits took 5 days. Generally, we spent 1 to 1.5 days interviewing and gathering data at the central district office; 2 to 2.5 days visiting schools, interviewing, and observing classrooms; and the remaining day interviewing various community representatives.

Each pair of field researchers paid observational visits to at least two schools and to central administrative offices, and interviewed school board members, administrators, teachers, parents, and community officials such as health and law enforcement officers. In the three largest districts (Washoe County, Clark County, and Fresno), a second visit of 2 to 4 more days was conducted in order to cover these districts more completely.

At the district level, about 10 interviews were scheduled. Researchers spoke with the superintendent, assistant superintendent, two school board members, one member of the district curriculum committee, one categorical services director, one special education director, one personnel director, the director of research and evaluation, and a school psychologist.

At the school level, about 10 interviews were scheduled per school, including the principal, vice principal, three teachers, one bilingual teacher, one ESL teacher, one community liaison, one parent, and one PTA officer. At the community level, interviews were scheduled when possible with child welfare or protective services social workers, one medical care provider, and one community historical librarian. Researchers also visited local libraries in search of historical documents. About 30 to 32 interviews were conducted per district for a total of 332 interviews.

Some interviews were conducted one-on-one; others paired the interviewers with one or two respondents at a time; and still others were group interviews with three to five respondents at a time. Site researchers had opportunities to attend faculty meetings, school board meetings, and other assemblies as these came up in the course of their visits.

A topical agenda provided an outline of the material to be covered in interviews with respondents. It included information about the respondent, the district's or school's students, district or school organization, and the political culture. A topical question guide provided conversational cues and information-gathering tips.

Site team members met after collecting interviews and observational data to review what they had learned, to plan how to divide work, and to determine the focus of the next day's agenda. At the close of days spent in selected schools, team members filled out the five rating scales (see the Appendix), compared their individual ratings, and developed a joint score on each item and on each overall scale.

We describe an actual case study visit to a small California district to give readers a flavor of what we experienced. After the initial contact with the district representative, we set up a schedule to meet with the superintendent and district administrators, and to visit specific schools.

On the first day, as a courtesy, we scheduled our first joint interview with the superintendent. We spent about an hour interviewing the superintendent, who was extremely cordial and personable and made us feel welcome. We attempted to arrange a lunch with him to establish a further connection, but in this case it was not possible, so we scheduled a follow-up meeting with him on our last day in the district.

We then interviewed other district administrators individually. The administrative staff appeared very competent and happy to be working in the district. They seemed supportive of the superintendent's program. We then interviewed two board members, one Hispanic and the other Anglo. Both were highly supportive of the superintendent, his program, and the schools. Neither rancor nor division was in any way apparent.

On the second and third day, we visited two local schools and spent most of the day there. We interviewed the principals, the vice principals, teachers—including bilingual teachers—one or two parents, a community liaison, and PTA officers. The principals were apparently handpicked by the superintendent. One school in particular was innovative in its practices, and we spent a lot of time there visiting classrooms and talking to teachers and students. We got the impression that teachers liked working in this district (and were quite highly paid, too).

On the fourth day, we interviewed a county social worker and a medical care provider and spent some time at a local library searching for historical documents. On the fifth day, we returned to the district site, where we finished up interviews and collected some fiscal and test achievement data. Our final discussion with the superintendent was very agreeable.

At no time did we feel that great differences of opinion existed in different areas of the district or at different levels of the hierarchy; the district seemed very cohesive. This was clearly an exemplary district (and a high performer), and we should note that most districts visited were not so easy to comprehend or analyze.

## DATA ANALYSIS

Each team was expected to prepare case reports according to an outline. Some teams tape-recorded their interviews and observations and exchanged the raw data with one another. Some teams divided the work of drafting their case report; others had one member draft it while the partner offered item contributions, review, and revisions.

The case reports included a general description of the district, sampled schools, district headquarters, and administrators obtained at the site visit. In addition, the reports gave detailed information on each school visited: educational approaches used, staff and material supports for students, learning outcomes, administrative approaches, parent involvement, and faculty and staff attitudes toward students and newcomers. A description of the district's political culture was also provided that included political climate, disposition, and values. In a conclusion, the writers assessed how demographic and economic changes, organizational features, and local history or political culture had facilitated or impeded the education of the district's disadvantaged students since 1980.

The case reports, recorded interviews, and observation notes, and the documentary materials gathered before and during each site visit, were filed for use of the analysts and co-authors. SWRL assigned a staff member independent of the project group to code the case reports. The coded report pages were then photocopied and filed under 29 topic headings to create a usable set of standardized files for cross-case comparisons. The topic headings, which were developed using the concepts and literature described in Chapter 1, included the following: bilingual education, immigrants, student achievement, student attitudes, teaching, educational programs, organization, budget, staff development, health and human service programs, school effectiveness, multiculturalism, poverty, and minorities (among others). Individual writers were assigned to cover various topics and sections of the final report.

Some of the methods of data analysis used in this study were triangulating, making contrasts and comparisons (high and low performers), and building a logical chain of evidence. After examining case study findings, we related these findings to each other and tried to identify patterns and the corresponding variables or constructs.

In reference to the validity of our findings, we used several tactics to test or confirm them (see Miles & Huberman, 1994, for a discussion). These included triangulating across data sources and methods, using extreme cases, and checking out rival explanations. Triangulation is a cross-validation tool used to corroborate findings. Generally we think of triangulating by data source, method, or type. In this study, sources included the superintendent, administrators, teachers, principals, school board members, students, parents, and community members. Various methods of data collection were employed, including interviews, use of school rating scales, student test scores, demographic information, school budgets, and classroom observations. Both qualitative and quantitative data were collected. This use of a wide array of data types and sources allowed us to get convergence on our findings.

We also used extreme cases, low and high performers, to help us verify our conclusions. We identified those districts that showed great improvement in scores over time, then looked at their attributes to help come up with general conclusions. We contrasted high performers with low performers.

Another tactic we used was checking out rival explanations for findings. We developed alternative hypotheses that might account for differences between low-performing and high-performing districts, analyzed the data to ascertain if they did make a difference, and reached a conclusion as to whether another variable might be at work. Correlations—or eyeballing the data—were used. For example, we thought that per capita spending on students in districts might account for variation in student outcomes. However, analysis showed that money did not differentiate between low- and high-performing districts. We also hypothesized that district size alone would determine outcomes. Yet two of the very large districts in our sample were stable performers, and only one was a low performer. No demographic variables used (percentage LEP, in poverty, and minority) significantly predicted change in achievement. School scale scores (Quality of Education and Quality of Teaching, in particular) did predict change in achievement over time, but not highly, and did have a rough correspondence with district rank as a high or low performer (with two anomalies).

The general internal validity or plausibility of our findings can be measured in different ways. First, triangulation and pattern-matching evidence provided generally convergent conclusions. The data presented validated the concepts proposed. Rival explanations were considered and discarded. In terms of external validity, generalizability can be made only to similar districts and not to all districts in the United States. Only districts in the West and with high demographic change were sampled. It may be possible to replicate the findings in similar impacted districts in other areas (e.g., Miami, New York City). The theory and concepts from the study should be generic enough to be transferable to other similar settings.

The study has several limitations that need to be kept in mind. These include limited availability of data, the representativeness of the sampled districts and sampled schools, comparability of different test scores, percentage of students tested by districts, and problems with reporting averages.

When we began this project, we looked forward to using a wide range of U.S. Census data. We planned to devise indicators of community workforce structures by ethnic composition as well as measures of household social characteristics and housing. The 1980 Census data were abundantly detailed and available, and these shaped our plans. The 1990 district detail data were not issued for California until late 1993, however; so at the onset we had to work from a more restricted data set. This reduced the power of the demographic variables in accounting for detailed differences between the communities. The Census demographic data have since been released and have been incorporated into this text.

In addition, we overestimated the extent to which school districts would preserve financial, personnel, and related records from the recent past. Many districts were unable to retrieve documents prior to 1984. Some could not go back that far. Thus our information on district budgets is limited.

The persons who carried out the field work had full knowledge of whether the district they were examining was a high- or a low-performing district. This knowledge could have biased their questions, perceptions, or interpretations of responses.

In reference to the representativeness of the sampled districts, the districts chosen purposively fall in the top quartile of demographic change for the three-state region. They are in that sense representative of those that had shown high demographic change, within the parameters used in this study (e.g., rural districts, very small districts, or those with fewer than 100 students per grade level were deleted). It is unclear whether the three large districts are representative of large districts only or of highly impacted districts in general. The small number of cases in this study cannot be treated as truly representative of all districts in the region or country.

An additional issue is whether the sampled schools within districts were representative of those districts. As previously noted, in two very large school districts, we were not allowed to choose the schools to be visited. In one of them, the district's staff chose schools that were for the most part brand new and probably not representative of the district's schools in general. In addition, this district is so large that selecting only three or four schools to "represent" the entire district would be difficult, if not impossible. Another large district also chose the schools for us, but these were clearly more typical for the district, as they displayed a great deal of diversity. For the remainder of the districts, we chose the schools to be visited on the basis of school demographic data. Thus most of the schools visited in those states were deemed to be representative of the districts.

Although we expected difficulties in developing a sound measure of the dependent variable, student achievement change over time, we discovered this task to be much harder even than we had anticipated. Most disappointing was our realization that too many districts lacked test score records for the years 1980 through 1983, forcing us to truncate our time period for measuring achievement to 1984 through 1990.

Lack of comparability of different tests across districts is a perennial problem. To mitigate this problem, we used change in achievement standard scores, because such scores can be compared across districts. In terms of measuring other standardized test scores to look at absolute rank, we used national percentiles in the belief that they should be comparable for the large standardized tests generally used (e.g., CTBS, CAT, ITBS).

Our study yielded no evidence to indicate that improved and more uniform and stable tests and measurements would be likely to improve the odds for school success for disadvantaged students. But they would certainly improve the prospects for good educational research.

Another factor that may be a source of error is that many schools in the study's sample either do not consistently test their LEP students or test only a small number because poor attendance or high transiency rates among LEP students reduce the number of these students available for being tested. This may lead to large population shifts in those tested from year to year. Some variation was seen in the percentage of students in a district who were actually tested by the state test. Moreover, some anecdotal evidence suggests that the percentages of LEP students reported by districts were higher than the percentages of these students actually tested. Thus using test scores alone to determine a district's effectiveness is a flawed measure, because the averages probably do not reflect the progress of many LEP students. As previously noted, since standardized achievement scores are limited assessments of students' knowledge and skills, we also used the five rating scales to measure school effectiveness.

Some limitations should be placed on interpretations made from the data presented. The data set contains school- and district-level information and no individual-level data. Both the demographic and achievement data represent district averages calculated from either household (Census) or school building (California Assessment Program [CAP], California Basic Education Data System [CBEDS], and Arizona State Department of Education [SDE]) data. By aggregating observations and using grouped means, the variation between individuals is lost, and important information about the distribution of student achievement is obscured. Basically, what is lost is the information on the variation of observations within groups (e.g., schools within districts).

Although these limitations prevent us from fully generalizing from the data, that was not our primary purpose in this study. We were looking for exemplary practices and evidence that certain policies, practices, or structures work in a certain type of situation. The data gathered were more than adequate for meeting our objectives and for answering our research questions. In particular, we found school districts with models of good practice and identified policies, practices, and structures that provide conditions for effectively hosting newcomer students.

Chapter 3 reviews differences in educational and instructional quality between high- and low-performing districts and integrates data on teaching staff. And in the remaining chapters, district indicators of conditions, processes, and programs that predict achievement gain and school effectiveness as measured by scales are explained. High-performing districts are compared and contrasted with low-performing districts on teaching-staff characteristics, instruction, educational programs, services provided, and organizational attributes.

# 3
# Clues to Quality: Staff, Instruction, and Programs

A school's instructional delivery system is an important component in measuring educational program quality and "success." According to our general approach described in Chapter 1, specific factors such as political culture and organizational structures can intervene between students' demographic predispositions and student outcomes. But what is actually experienced each day in classrooms between teaching staff and students can also greatly influence the outcomes of an educational system.

Educational research has been somewhat successful in identifying key instructional strategies, programs, and curricula that address the needs of today's disadvantaged and culturally and linguistically diverse students. Figure 3.1 is a summary of our version of the components and indicators of an ideal instructional delivery system. We constructed this figure and its components prior to the study using both theoretical and applied research evidence (see Figure 3.1 for literature citations). In addition, we used our team's observations in this project to add desirable indicators to this system.

The basic components are drawn from Shavelson, McDonnell, Oakes, Carey, and Picus's (1987) linking elements of the educational system. In an input–process–output model, Shavelson et al. view the "input" components as fiscal and other resources, teacher quality, school quality, and student background. Components of "processes" include curriculum quality, teaching quality, and instructional quality, and components of "outputs" are achievement, participation, and attitudes.

The system used here includes only input and process elements: teacher characteristics and teacher quality; school quality, including standards and assessments and instructional organization; instructional quality, including strategies and approaches, and access to second-language and other programs for the disadvantaged. The guiding principles in this system are equal access to a core curriculum, equal opportunities to learn, and the belief that all children can learn, regardless of background. Within each

## Figure 3.1  Components and Indicators in an Ideal Instructional Delivery System

**Teacher Characteristics and Teacher Quality** *(Fullan, 1990; Olsen & Mullen, 1990)*
- Teachers qualified in field
- Teachers' ethnic/linguistic profiles match children's
- Effective staff development
- Positive attitudes and morale

### School Quality

*Standards & Assessments (McLaughlin, Shepard, & O'Day, 1995)*
- Achievement outcomes-focused
- Authentic classroom assessment
- Shared vision of instructional goals
- High expectations for all children

*Instructional Organization (Elmore & McLaughlin, 1988; Oakes, 1990)*
- Equal access to core curriculum
- Grade-level and subject articulation
- Flexible groupings
- Team teaching
- No tracking, ability grouping
- Peer and cross-age tutoring
- Collaborative planning, decision making

### Instructional Quality

*Strategies & Approaches (Brophy & Good, 1986)*
- Basic, advanced skills taught through meaningful tasks
- Use of manipulatives, realia
- Connections made with students' cultures
- Active student participation
- Literature-based and holistic

*Access to Second Language Programs (Garcia, 1992; Berman et al., 1992)*
- Comprehensive bilingual program
- ESL or sheltered instruction program
- Primary-language materials available
- Sufficient number of bilingual teachers and aides
- Students' primary language to build comprehension
- English language development integrated

*Access to Chapter 1 Programs (Means et al., 1991; Birman et al., 1987)*
- Schoolwide or in-class arrangements
- Common program and objectives
- Peer tutoring
- Tutoring/mentoring
- Cooperative learning groups

component, key references and ideal indicators are listed. It should be noted that although much of the research literature supports these indicators, some of the characteristics remain controversial (for example, characteristics of second-language programs).

This chapter focuses on the three major components of our ideal instructional delivery system: teacher quality, school quality, and instructional quality. School quality and teacher quality are seen as inputs to the educational system, whereas instructional quality components (including strategies and approaches and access to second-language and Chapter 1 programs) are seen as processes. Throughout the chapter, high-performing districts are compared and contrasted with low-performing and stable districts on the indicators in the ideal instructional system. Districts are also compared on the Quality of Teaching and Quality of Education scale scores. A brief conclusion and summary table end the chapter.

## TEACHER CHARACTERISTICS AND TEACHER QUALITY

The challenges the sampled districts faced often manifested themselves in ways that affected teacher quality and teachers' working conditions adversely. For example, in many districts visited we found large class sizes, a lack of teaching materials in students' native languages, few trained paraprofessionals or parent volunteers who could provide primary-language support to language minority students, and resource specialists, counselors, and social workers who were stretched to their professional limits and could provide only limited support to teachers. But as we report in this chapter, these conditions were not universal, and in high-performing districts, teachers often were able to cope effectively with less than ideal circumstances.

We do not discuss the districts' organizational and policy responses in detail here, but we do discuss them in Chapter 5. However, one point is worth noting in the context of districts' teaching staffs. Without exception, the demographic shifts experienced by the districts we studied were not short term—that is, over 2 or 3 years—but rather occurred over a long period (8 to 15 years). Long-term trends were obvious, especially in districts close to the United States/Mexico border. Each year, there were more non-English-speaking or limited-English-proficient students and more economically disadvantaged students. Changes in U.S. immigration laws in the mid-1980s brought an influx of language minority and poor children from Mexico. Therefore, over time it would be possible to engage in long-term planning and to implement proactive strategies to address future enrollment projections. In short, it was possible to take charge of change (Hord, Rutherford, Huling-Austin, & Hall, 1987).

High-performing districts modified their policies and programs over time to address the changing needs of their students. For example, over a 7-year period from 1985 to 1992, the sample district that showed the greatest achievement gain (Isaac, Arizona) moved from delivering a very conventional, poorly funded program of multicultural education and human relations to delivering an unconventional, better funded and managed program of multicultural instruction and human relations.

What distinguished the teaching staffs in more effective districts from those in less effective districts? Overall, teachers in high-performing districts taught in districtwide settings characterized by policy and programmatic responses to changing student demographics that, in turn, supported their daily classroom activities and kept their morale and optimism high. Districts that recognized and reacted to changing demographics as they occurred used the following strategies to equip their teaching staffs and, ultimately, to benefit their students:

- Recruiting and hiring bilingual and minority teachers to narrow the gap between teachers' and students' cultural and linguistic profiles.
- Providing teachers with effective staff development.
- Transmitting to teachers positive attitudes toward changing demographics and positive expectations for students' performance and success.

In the sections that follow, we discuss each of these three strategies.

## Narrowing the Gap

Without exception, all the districts we studied employed lower percentages of minority teachers than were desirable given the growing and, in many cases, high representation of minority students among their student enrollments. An issue of national concern as fewer minorities enter teaching (Justiz & Kameen, 1988; Olsen & Mullen, 1990; Spellman, 1988), this "mismatch" between student and teacher demographics is particularly acute in the Pacific Southwest (i.e., Arizona, California, and Nevada) where students are more ethnically and linguistically diverse than in any other region of the country, but their teachers are predominantly Anglo. For example, California's teachers remain 82% Anglo, almost unchanged from a decade ago (California Department of Education, 1993). Approximately 86% of Arizona's teachers and 90% of Nevada's teachers are Anglo ("Embracing Diversity," 1992).

The mismatch between teacher and student demographics adversely affects educational quality to the extent that students are taught by individuals who cannot serve as racial/ethnic role models, do not share students' cultural heritage, and often cannot speak students' primary or native languages. Therefore, they cannot provide instruction in those languages or mediate instruction in English based on their facility with students' primary languages. This last point is especially relevant in the Pacific Southwest, particularly in California, the region's most diverse state. Berman et al. (1992) report that only half of California's Spanish-speaking students are taught by a teacher who speaks Spanish. Among other language groups, only 10% to 20% of students are taught by teachers who speak the students' languages.

The serious and continuing shortage of bilingual teachers in California is approaching crisis proportions. With nearly 1 in 5 students speaking little or no English, the state has approximately 8,000 teachers with bilingual teaching credentials and another 4,000 who are not bilingual, but are credentialed to help students acquire English-language skills. Together, these 12,000 teachers fill less than half the state's need for bilingual teachers (Lambert, 1991).

But other Western region states are feeling similar pressures. With fewer than 1,000 bilingual credentialed teachers in 1989–90, one credentialed bilingual teacher was available for every 74 LEP students enrolled in Arizona schools that year (Hafner & Green, 1992). The least diverse of the Western region states, Nevada does not currently grant a bilingual credential. In contrast, California is replacing its current bilingual credential and its language development specialist certificate with a new basic emphasis credential that acknowledges the increasingly multicultural and multilingual nature of the state's students (California Commission on Teacher Credentialing, 1992).

Table 3.1 illustrates how the districts we studied mirror these regional trends. The districts are grouped according to changes in achievement (e.g., high performers, stable, low performers). On average, 22% of teachers and 70% of students were ethnic minority group members. On average, about 30% of students in sample districts were LEP.

Most of the Arizona and California districts were majority-minority districts (those in which minority group members are the majority). We have noted the percentage of LEP students in each district, although simple "percent LEP" hides great diversity in some districts, where students come to school speaking Mandarin, Cantonese, Hmong, Lao, Cambodian, Vietnamese, Tagalog, Filipino, Polish, Arabic, or a host of other primary languages. Districts such as Rosemead, National, Franklin McKinley, Sunnyside, and Mountain View serve almost exclusively minority student populations.

In contrast, the two Nevada districts were only beginning to experience the large demographic shifts in enrollment common in the other two

**Table 3.1  Percentage of Minority Teachers and Students in Study's Districts**

| Achievement Change | District | Percentage Minority Teachers | Percentage Minority Students |
|---|---|---|---|
| High performers | Isaac AZ | 21 | 79 (33% LEP) |
| | Rosemead CA | 14 | 87 (26% LEP) |
| | National CA | 35 | 90 (30% LEP) |
| Stable performers | Franklin McK CA | 29 | 88 (24% LEP) |
| | Washoe Co. NV | 5 | 21 (5% LEP) |
| | Clark Co. NV | 19 | 32 (5% LEP) |
| | Balsz AZ | 8 | 54 (11% LEP) |
| Low performers | San Gabriel CA | 16 | 75 (29% LEP) |
| | Fresno CA | 19 | 67 (20% LEP) |
| | Sunnyside AZ | 28 | 71 (13% LEP) |
| | Mt. View CA | 51 | 96 (40% LEP) |

states. For example, in the Washoe School District minority enrollment doubled in the last decade but still accounts for only 21% of the student population. Similarly, LEP students are only 5% of its population. Not unexpectedly, the district has very few minority or bilingual teachers at this time. Over the past decade, Clark County showed a large growth in minority and LEP student population and began to recognize the need to train more teachers in ESL techniques and to put a more ethnically diverse staff in its schools. Almost one third of its students are now minority, and 5% are LEP students. Owing to recruitment efforts, almost 20% of the district's teachers are now minority group members.

High-performing districts used recruitment and personnel strategies to narrow the gap between the racial, ethnic, and linguistic makeup of their teachers and students. These districts worked to increase the numbers of bilingual or specially certificated teachers (e.g., language development specialist). Superintendents placed a high priority on hiring bilingual teachers, often interviewing candidates themselves. But this step was not sufficient. As Table 3.1 illustrates, high-performing districts such as National had many minority teachers, a substantial portion of whom had taught in the district for years, long before the newcomer Latino students began to arrive. Although mainly Hispanic, these veteran teachers sometimes reported feeling a lack of identity with the economically disadvantaged newcomer students from Mexico.

A low-performing district, Mountain View, mounted an intense recruitment effort over the last decade to increase minority representation among its teaching staff, so that by 1992, approximately half of its teachers were members of a racial or ethnic minority. In this district we found teachers who were recruited specifically to educate newcomer students, and who were sensitive to their students' needs but frustrated in their efforts to be effective by organizational factors outside their control.

A second step proved critical in effective recruitment and hiring. High-performing districts made broad-ranging staff changes as part of programmatic and policy changes that positioned the districts to deal with changing student demographics. Within this broader programmatic and policy context, staffing changes demonstrated visibly to teachers the district's commitment to deliver effective services to children. Isaac provides an excellent example of fundamental shifts that positioned the district well for meeting the needs of its changing student population. The Isaac School District underwent a profound transformation between 1985 and 1992, including sweeping changes in personnel, programs, and planning. The district's hiring strategy was integral to its success. Because of it, each school now has larger numbers of bilingual teachers, administrators, and teachers' aides. About 20% of the district's teachers are minority. Over the past decade, the number of certified staff in the district with bilingual endorsements or provisional endorsements increased from 3 to 26. Some 83 bilingual teachers were hired in the last 4 years, about 78 of whom are Spanish bilingual.

Third, high-performing districts used either monetary incentives or the excellent reputations of their bilingual programs to attract minority and bilingual teachers. With respect to incentives, Isaac pays a supplement to teachers with bilingual certification. It also has one of the highest teacher pay scales in Arizona, a strong incentive for teachers' attraction to and continued employment in any district (Murnane, Singer, Willett, Kemple, & Olsen, 1991). San Gabriel, one of the low-performing districts, complained that bilingual teachers could pick and choose among the places they would like to go and thus more often select districts that pay more than San Gabriel does.

Another high-performing district, Rosemead, augmented its competitive teacher salaries with a $500 cash incentive provided to any newly hired or currently employed teacher who takes additional courses and passes a state-administered exam required for additional certification as an English language development (ELD) specialist. However, although Rosemead administrators said they placed a high value on hiring bilingual teachers, only 7% of the district's teachers are bilingual. The district does have a reasonable number of ethnic minority teachers and many bilingual aides. By contrast, a neighboring district, San Gabriel, was not in an economic position to offer such an incentive and instead merely required new hires to sign an agreement that they would complete the ELD certificate some-time during the first 3 years of their contract.

Taking a different approach, another high-performing district, National, attracted teachers because of the excellent reputation of its bilingual pro-gram. Forty percent of the teachers in National held bilingual certificates, and the district reported few recruitment problems. In the 2 or 3 years before our study, National had hired bilingual and special education teach-ers exclusively.

Still, aggressive recruiting, competitive teacher salaries, special finan-cial incentives, and strong programs that attract bilingual teachers were not sufficient to solve high-performing districts' staffing shortages. All continued to have shortages of bilingual and/or ESL teachers. However, when they could not fill all the positions they needed—which proved an extraordinary challenge, especially in the California districts with multi-lingual student populations—they augmented their teaching staff with trained paraprofessionals. These individuals often spoke students' primary languages and could provide instruction in these languages and in English, thus enabling students to acquire academic content and make the transi-tion to English (Cummins & McNeely, 1987).

Rosemead provides the best example of this strategy. Rosemead dif-fers from National and Isaac, which are predominantly Hispanic districts, in its large Asian population (34%). The district tries to recruit teachers who reflect the ethnic groups in the community; however, this has proved difficult given the general shortage of teachers who speak the languages the district needs. Finding qualified teachers in all of the students' primary languages is impossible, and there are still major shortages of teachers who speak Vietnamese, Cambodian, and Mandarin. Therefore, trained para-professionals, who speak these languages, became integral to the educa-tional program. The district has assigned ESL teachers and aides to its schools, in addition to its bilingual teachers. The same is true in Isaac, where trained paraprofessionals are used in most elementary classrooms. How-ever, National and Isaac school districts have intentionally chosen to re-place their numerous bilingual aides with a greater number of bilingual teachers.

In low-performing districts, we found few bilingual teachers and few minority teachers, with two exceptions: Sunnyside, with 28% minority teachers, and Mountain View, with 51% minority and 35% bilingual teach-ers. In most low-performing districts, we found an absence of trained para-professionals and, in some cases, an approach in which schools could al-locate their own funds to hiring these individuals if they chose to expend funds this way. However, there was no districtwide pressure to do so.

## Providing Effective Staff Development

Researchers have established a link between effective staff development, successful innovation, and school achievement (Fullan & Pomfret, 1977; Fullan, 1990). As important, we know a great deal about what effective staff development looks like (Fullan, 1990; Guskey & Huberman, 1995). The only problem is that staff development seldom looks this way, much to teachers' frustration (Eisner, 1992). According to Fullan (1990), at least two reasons account for the poor quality of staff development. The first is technical; it takes a lot of expertise and persistence to design and implement effective staff development efforts. The second is political. Because staff development is big business, with large budgets, it is as much related to power, bureaucratic positioning, and territoriality as it is to helping teachers and students.

In their comprehensive review of staff development in California, Little et al. (1987) found that staff development resources were deployed in ways that reinforced existing patterns of teaching, conventional structures of schools, and long-standing traditions in teaching. Equally important, the state had no comprehensive or consistent policy position with respect to staff development or the institutions that provide it, including local school districts. Consequently, Little et al. concluded that staff development activities and incentives were unlikely to change teachers' thinking or performance substantially.

We found that only two sample districts, Isaac and National, had overcome these technical and political barriers and, moreover, that they were successful in providing teachers with the specific form of staff development demanded by the districts' demographic shifts. In the Isaac School District, these shifts were so dramatic that teachers needed assistance to internalize high expectations for groups of students they had not previously taught; to understand the relationship between students' learning and their home and cultural backgrounds, which were so frequently different from those of the teachers; and to fit a range of instructional approaches into a new conception of their teaching role. These needs required staff development that was comprehensive, focused, and sustained, and that provided teachers with the time, support, and information necessary for them to learn, practice, and experience success with new instructional strategies and approaches. Its domain is the culture of the school as a workplace and its focus is on increasing schools' capacity and performance for continuous improvement (Fullan, 1990; Little, 1982; Rosenholtz, 1989; Sarason, 1982).

In Isaac, staff development occurred within the context of site-based management, which, in turn, occurred in a broader district context in which LEP students were the primary educational focus. Site-based management addressed basic issues of school culture and collaborative relationships and responsibility among faculties. In this context, staff development was not imposed by the district; instead, school staffs were provided with district and school training opportunities, and most chose voluntarily to participate. For example, federal Title VII funds were used to provide staff development classes for bilingual teachers. The district provided certification classes for teachers interested in obtaining bilingual endorsements. Teachers also were supported with school-based skills-training forums funded from a Title VII grant through which English-speaking teachers could attain bilingual proficiency. In the National School District, as in Isaac, district staff development occurred within the context of site-based management and operated in tandem with school-site staff development.

High-performing districts were distinguished from low-performing districts by sustained central office support of teachers' continuous learning, most visibly by the operation of professional development centers (PDCs). For example, National has operated a PDC since 1986, through which it periodically cycles all teaching personnel to update and refresh teaching skills and techniques. This PDC is dedicated to staying abreast of current teaching/learning research and empowering teachers with new strategies. Teachers also receive advanced training at regional universities and seminars. Many language-arts teachers have been trained in the California Literature Project, and every National teacher receives 20 hours of training by the UC San Diego California Writing Project staff. The PDC's goals are to improve teacher instructional skills, to broaden the teacher knowledge base of learning theory and its applications, to stimulate teacher interest in continued professional growth and development, and to promote the value of collaborative effort. The district also delivered an extensive staff development program in bilingual education. The teachers with whom we spoke expressed satisfaction with, and spoke highly about, training and workshops provided for their PDC.

Districts other than high-performing ones also operated PDCs, but with less success. Stable performer Washoe County has had a PDC since 1985; however, budget cuts allow the center only one full-time trainer, which greatly inhibits its effectiveness. Even though it has not been operating at peak efficiency, Washoe's PDC has tried to deliver one kind of training well, namely, staff development for the district's Chapter 1 teachers, which connected to the district's efforts to revamp its Chapter 1 program. As a result, the center's training was focused and sustained. Under the district's emerging ESL strategy, it hopes to use funds it wins competitively to add staff to the center so it can train teachers in sheltered content instruction.

In contrast, some of the low-performing districts engaged in many different kinds of staff development activities, most of which were symptomatic of the districts' constantly changing priorities and efforts to try new reforms in the hopes that something would work. Some researchers have identified this approach to delivering staff development as particularly detrimental to effective change (Loucks-Horsley et al., 1987; Pink, 1989). Sunnyside, for example, moved within 10 years from mastery learning, to cooperative learning, to Assertive Discipline, which was replaced by Reality Therapy, which, in turn, gave way to Reading Recovery. Each reform was accompanied by a new wave of staff development delivered by high-priced trainers from outside the district. In Sunnyside we found teachers who were not only confused but cynical and angry about changing priorities that translated into yet another series of required workshops, which did little to help teachers improve their own performance or the performance of their students

But not all the stable or low-performing districts implemented poor staff development. Balsz did not even offer staff development training until 3 years ago, when a new director of curriculum was hired. Now teachers are provided with content and instructional support through in-service sessions. The district also offers small cash and credit incentives to participating teachers. Training sessions target linguistic and cultural minority issues. Many have been provided by the district; others are offered in conjunction with a nearby university.

Similarly, not all the high-performing districts implemented exemplary staff development. In Rosemead, for example, staff development is a 30–hour, district-sponsored training program on techniques and methods for English-language acquisition at which teacher attendance is voluntary. The training program supports a recent change in the district's bilingual program and is part of the district's evolving efforts to be responsive to students' needs. Although they acknowledged the program as a good beginning, teachers told us they needed much more staff development to enable them to meet the needs of a diverse student population.

## Transmitting Positive Attitudes

The power of teacher expectations has been well documented in the research literature (Brophy & Good, 1986; Means et al., 1991). Expectations are inferences teachers make about the future academic achievement of their students and, as a consequence, about the types of classroom assignments students should be given in light of their abilities. Our interest was not in the processes individual teachers used to form their expectations but rather in how districts' expectations influenced teachers. Districts' expectations for students are expressed as policies and programs and ulti-mately filter down to classroom teachers.

High-performing districts differed from low-performing districts in their unfailingly positive attitude toward changing student demographics. In contrast, administrators in low-performing districts often complained about how difficult the "new" students were to educate. And, in many cases, they were correct. For example, some of the districts close to the U.S./Mexican border experienced a wave of newcomer students from extremely impov-erished families. Children often entered school with no formal schooling or interrupted schooling. Immigrant children from Asia include those with formal schooling as well as those from poor villages without schools. For example, Hmong children speak a language that until recently had no written lexicon. In some stable and low-performing districts, a strong "En-glish only" movement became prominent, and attitudes against multi-cultural education were evident.

We found a "can do" attitude and optimism among the high-performing districts that they could provide effective services for even their most dis-advantaged students. This attitude, in turn, was reflected in high teacher expectations and high teacher morale. Teachers came to understand that children who are poor and who are from culturally and linguistically dif-ferent backgrounds bring with them to school unlimited potential and an impressive set of intellectual accomplishments. As a result, they were positioned to take steps to reshape the curriculum and apply new instruc-tional strategies to enable all children to succeed (Means et al., 1991; Slavin, Dolan, Madden, Karweit, & Wasik, 1992).

In Isaac, for example, the changes in household and student demo-graphic composition in the last decade were completely accepted as natu-ral, appropriate, and a development that the administrative team was proud of having planned for and responded to programmatically. School staffs intended to transform their programs, believed they were doing so, and exhibited high morale.

Similarly, the administrative staff in the National School District had a positive attitude about the changes there and felt confident they were handling the challenges posed. Almost everyone interviewed remarked on the strong commitment shown by district staff. Teachers were excited about what they were doing with children. They had high expectations and felt they were making progress with their students. Also, we found teacher morale high despite high student poverty, overcrowded classrooms, funding cuts, and the special instructional needs of a multilingual student population. No one commented negatively on the presence of immigrant or newly arriving students.

In Rosemead, we also found district administrators with positive attitudes toward demographic changes. Teachers, administrators, and school staff were supportive, committed, and enthusiastic about providing safe, orderly, and caring learning environments that reflected an academic focus and high expectations for student achievement and behavior. Teacher morale was high even within a context of overcrowded classrooms and enormous student diversity. School administrators and teachers viewed students' multiculturalism as one of the district's strongest assets.

## SCHOOL QUALITY

Within the School Quality category, as shown in Figure 3.1, are the components of standards and assessments and instructional organization. Districts that reacted proactively to changing demographics used the following explicit policies and strategies to support their students and teachers:

- Providing equal access to a core curriculum by avoiding tracking and ability grouping and using flexible grouping methods.
- Promoting team teaching and grade-level and subject articulation by fostering teacher collaboration and involvement in planning and decision making.
- Holding a shared vision of instructional goals that included high expectations of students and focused on student outcomes and assessments.

In the following sections, we describe explicitly how high-performing districts showed indicators of school quality in the three areas of providing equal access, fostering teacher collaboration, and holding a shared vision reinforced with appropriate assessments. In addition, patterns in low-performing and stable districts are compared and contrasted with those in high-performing districts.

### Providing Equal Access to a Core Curriculum

High-performing districts often had an explicit policy of equal access to the core curriculum. This ensures that certain children, regardless of special status, do not miss out on any curricular or content areas that the regular program offers to all other children. This is especially important for special-needs and LEP children. National, for example, holds equal access to be a key factor in district planning. The concept was incorporated into all school plans and program quality reviews. In addition, the district has a textbook adoption program that maintains parity. In other words, if an English text is adopted, a similar text is adopted for use by Spanish speakers. The percentage of money spent on English and Spanish textbooks is equal to the percentage of students in each language group.

In the Isaac School District, program changes in the past 10 years provided improved academic learning opportunities to all groups. They included new strategies for building self-esteem, participating in leadership and community service, and reaching out to parents. The historically outstanding varsity athletic program at the junior high has been opened up, for example, to give equal emphasis and resources to girls' teams.

In stable and low-performing districts, large groups of children, especially special education students with individual education plans (IEPs) and LEP students, were deprived of full access to the core academic subjects. This was especially true in such unified districts as Fresno and Washoe County, at the junior high and high school levels. Many newcomer students in these districts were placed in remedial or "individualized" instruction classes and were not taught the subject matter that regular students were required to learn.

In a remedial English class we visited in a Fresno high school, a student led the class in a discussion of a story, only to eventually explode in frustration at the other students' lack of response to his questions. Speaking primarily in excellent English, and occasionally in Spanish, he asked the class some questions about the story. When no one answered, he ranted: "You guys are illiterate in English *and* Spanish." The students looked around at each other, stunned. Only a fellow student would say something like that, but the looks on their faces showed that they realized some truth in what he said. The low level of instruction given to many LEP students in such remedial classes does not provide them with high opportunities to become literate, as regular classes do.

High-performing districts and some stable districts tended to avoid tracking and ability grouping. They also tended to deemphasize gifted and talented programs. This was especially true in the elementary schools we visited. National had a gifted program, but it was available to everyone, and many minority group students participated. The district also had a bilingual gifted program.

In low-performing districts, widespread tracking was seen, especially in junior high and high schools. Even in elementary schools, in which all children received the same core subjects, many were grouped by reading or math ability. None of these districts had policies against tracking or ability grouping and in fact seemed to prefer differentiating among high and low scorers, so as to "serve these groups better." In some cases, statistics on the ethnic makeup of gifted and talented programs showed very low proportions of minority group and LEP students.

High-performing districts had a decided tendency to use flexible grouping methods such as heterogeneous ability grouping or multi-age (nongraded) classrooms. In Isaac, in nongraded primary classrooms, an English teacher and a bilingual teacher would rotate between different groups at different ends of the room. Teamwork between the teachers was clearly planned but not rigid. Children were allowed to progress at their own rates and grade retention was avoided.

In low-performing or stable districts, we saw no multi-age or nongraded classrooms. In addition, few flexible grouping methods were used. Although we observed ability grouping, it was usually in the context of same-level ability. Two of the low-performing districts (Sunnyside and Mountain View) did use flexible grouping methods to some degree.

## Fostering Teacher Collaboration, Planning, and Decision Making

Although the districts we studied varied in the effectiveness with which they educated academically disadvantaged students even before the demographic changes, these changes and their accompanying increase in the enrollment of such students put greater demands on teachers and administrators. In fact, the sheer numbers of academically disadvantaged students, either in absolute terms or as a percentage increase, forced districts to face change and to adapt. High-performing districts made more effective adaptations; low-performing districts were either slow to change or seemed to change all the time, moving from one quick fix or educational fad to the next.

Ultimately the changes the districts sought to make were implemented by teachers. And the literature is clear about what it takes for teachers to improve and change practice collectively. They (and, as a consequence, their schools) change when they have (a) a shared purpose; (b) norms of collegiality; (c) norms of continuous change and improvement; and (d) structures that represent organizational conditions necessary for significant change (Elmore & McLaughlin, 1988; Little et al., 1987; Rosenholtz, 1989).

Our focus here is on norms of collegiality, collaboration, and continuous change. Collegiality is defined as the "extent to which mutual sharing, assistance, and joint work among teachers is valued and honored in the school" (Fullan, 1990, p. 17). There is nothing particularly virtuous about collaboration per se. In fact, it can block change as well as encourage it (Hargreaves & Dawe, 1989). As Fullan (1990) points out, the criti-

cal issue is the linkage to norms of continuous improvement and experimentation in which teachers constantly seek and assess better practices
within and outside their schools. Development of a professional network
in schools helps to alleviate the isolation of classroom teachers. It can expand teachers' ideas of what can be done, help them recognize their own
expertise, and help build awareness of important issues.

In this area, high-performing districts contrasted markedly with the
low-performing districts, in which we found almost no teacher collaboration or, at best, pockets of teacher collaboration. One example of such a
pocket was in Sunnyside, where the district's bilingual teachers teamed
and collaborated under the leadership of an especially dedicated bilingual
education coordinator in the district's central office. High-performing districts exhibited a high level of teacher collaboration and program planning, including team teaching, mentoring, and use of grade-level and
sometimes subject-matter articulation. Articulation refers to teachers'
(either those at a specific grade level or who teach a specific subject matter) meeting together on a regular basis to align their teaching content or
strategies. This may involve coordinating courses, lesson plans, or themes.
For example, teachers in exemplary schools and districts had an intimate
knowledge of the topics, themes, and skills being taught each week by other
teachers at their grade level or in their department (articulation is most
often seen at the elementary level). Teachers talked frequently together
about teaching, strategies and practices, and subject-matter knowledge.
They occasionally observed each others' classes and sometimes switched
classes.

National and Rosemead provide excellent examples of teacher collaboration within the broader context of school improvement and innovation.
In the National School District, each grade-level teacher had a team partner or partners at the same level with whom he or she coordinated courses
and planned lessons. Teachers shared curriculum materials, instructional
ideas, academic goals, and their knowledge of subject-matter content with
each other. In a spirit of experimentation to find the best way to serve
students, teachers reported they felt free to use suggestions and ideas offered by their colleagues. They actively sought better ideas from other
schools in the district, from university staff, and from their own readings.
When we visited one school in National, the third-grade teachers were
using the theme of change in all their classrooms. Teachers had different
displays showing various aspects of change in nature over time, and they
took turns taking various students through them.

In Rosemead, teachers also organized themselves into grade-level teams
in which they worked cooperatively. Especially within grade level, teachers were aware of what others were doing, and we found a great deal of

sharing and articulation among them. Like teachers in National, teachers in Rosemead actively sought out new teaching approaches and materials, and they were encouraged by their principals to experiment and innovate.

Some high-performing districts (e.g., National and Isaac) instituted new organizational schemes, such as site-based decision making, that were conducive to collaboration (Shanker, 1990). And they backed this organizational change with strong support for teacher collaboration and experimentation. In the Isaac School District, teachers and other staff enjoyed great autonomy and self-determination of programs and division of labor. Building staffs really ran their schools, and veteran and new teachers alike trusted and worked smoothly with one another and with administrators. Teachers were respected as professionals and given considerable autonomy over their classes, opportunities to participate in curricular decision making, and chances to work with each other.

In low-performing districts, teachers generally worked in isolation and did not seem to know what other teachers were doing. Overall, they were unaware of other teachers' strategies, methods, or topics. Some stable and low-performing districts, however, showed some evidence of teacher collaboration. For example, in Mountain View teachers frequently worked in teams, making plans regarding topics and themes. Bilingual teachers met fairly often with monolingual English teachers to coordinate lesson planning. Balsz also showed some elements of teachers' working together in a collaborative way. Although Washoe County, in general, operated under a very traditional approach that included teachers' working in isolation, one elementary school offered an exception. The arrival of a new superintendent 3 years ago set the stage for a new accountability focus that made possible the creation of a site-based management pilot program at this school. Here we saw elements of teachers' working together with the principal and parents to plan the school's program.

## Holding a Shared Vision and Using Appropriate Assessments

Districts that responded proactively to the changing demographics used assessment-and-standards–focused strategies that supported their students and promoted higher outcomes. They had explicit objectives, showed high expectations for all children, used authentic classroom assessment, and focused on student outcomes. They shared a common, widely promoted vision of instructional goals and generally had a philosophy of elementary education rooted in cognitive psychology. A capacity-building model, rather than a deficit model, was evident. The superintendent, administrators, principals, and teachers shared in these beliefs and goals and supported the district vision. For example, in Isaac, the district staff and superintendent were unified around very strongly expressed educational and social goals, and administrators were explicitly delegated the authority and given the autonomy to implement these goals.

In the other districts, instructional goals were not articulated. Traditional approaches dominated. There were, however, a couple of exceptions. For example, Washoe County developed a consensus document that is a long-range plan for the district, which includes instructional goals. However, it had not been promoted or implemented at the time of our study.

In terms of using assessments, some of the districts were employing portfolios, journals, and other methods of measuring authentic assessment. High-performing districts did not always participate in such activities but had a general openness to the idea that we did not observe in other districts. The National School District had recently been training teachers in using language-arts portfolios. Teachers began using them in fall 1992 in the area of reading. Eventually, the district plans to add writing, social science, and science. The district also recently developed a new report card that is nongraded and performance-based. The portfolio will be used in conjunction with the new report card to show student progress. The district is working to get away from exclusive use of standardized tests.

In Isaac, hands-on testing strategies in the sciences have begun to supplant abstract, text-based instruction and assessment. Creative and performing arts activities and projects were used extensively and were of high quality. Isaac continues to use state performance assessment materials in English and Spanish.

In some low-performing and stable districts, we saw some scattered evidence of authentic assessment and focus on student outcomes. Balsz and Sunnyside in Arizona were using the state's performance assessment materials in English and Spanish. In most other low-performing districts, traditional types of assessment were evident.

## INSTRUCTIONAL QUALITY:
## STRATEGIES AND APPROACHES

In the United States, extreme gaps in achievement between low and high socioeconomic status (SES) youth are the norm. The correlation between SES and academic achievement is well documented (Lee, 1986). Although SES accounts for a substantial proportion of the variation in explaining achievement (Hoffer, Greeley, & Coleman, 1985), it is probable that educational programs and instructional variables may be more important than previously recognized (Brophy & Good, 1986). Researchers attribute low performance to various other causes, including grouping students by ability (tracking); a repetitive, skill-based curriculum; unequal opportunities for students to learn; and teacher beliefs and attitudes about student abilities. Although all of these "causes" are of concern, explanations that rely on the nature of teacher and classroom instruction for differential student achievement are among those most prominent today (Hafner, 1993).

According to some theorists, effective instruction of ethnolinguistically diverse students requires teachers to integrate content knowledge acquisition and English-language development (Garcia, 1992). This means that teachers must use instructional practices that will help increase students' academic performance and also that teachers' knowledge, abilities, and activities must meet diverse students' particular learning needs.

Key instructional strategies that address the needs of culturally diverse students (and, indeed, the needs of all students) have been identified in the literature (see Berman et al., 1992; Collier, 1992; Garcia, 1992). Research in the cognitive-science and at-risk/disadvantaged population areas has converged on the identification of these effective and ineffective strategies. The effective strategies listed in Figure 3.2 are practices that all good teachers could follow.

**Figure 3.2. Effective and Ineffective Instructional Strategies for Teaching Students**

| *Effective* | *Ineffective* |
|---|---|
| • Student oriented | • Teacher-oriented |
| • Active student participation | • Passive reception of teacher talk |
| • Outcomes focused | • Focus on delivery of instruction |
| • Language acquired in natural contexts | • Language learned in isolated contexts |
| • Emphasis on meaning and function | • Excessive emphasis on form over meaning |
| • Socially appropriate ways of communicating culture | • Superficial presentation of cultural issues and symbols |
| • Equal treatment and access for all to instruction for high level comprehension | • Use of differential content and teaching strategies based on ability, language |
| • Cooperative learning in heterogeneous groups | • Individual learning and/or competition |
| • Use of manipulatives and realia to teach principles and concepts | • Exclusive focus on abstract rules, principles |
| • Basic and advanced skills and key concepts taught through meaningful tasks | • "Basics" taught as isolated facts and discrete skills |

The philosophy of social constructivism proposes that knowledge is acquired as a result of students' interacting socially with the teacher and the subject matter to create meaning and learning. Discovery and cooperative learning are key concepts. Overall, effective strategies are outcomes-focused, encourage active student participation, focus on meaning and function, and use cooperative learning as well as realia and manipulatives. Ineffective strategies are teacher-oriented, focus on delivery of instruction and teacher talk, competition, abstract rules and principles, and emphasize form and style, facts, and discrete skills. Basically, it is proposed here that the "effective" strategies can be used effectively with any students, not just those who are culturally diverse (Garcia, 1992; Hafner, 1993; Means et al., 1991).

To ascertain the overall educational quality of the districts' instructional delivery system, we examined scores on the Quality of Teaching (QT) and the Quality of Education (QE) scales. As discussed in Chapter 2, the QT scale involves academic press, use of a variety of teaching strategies, support for in-service education, cooperation among teachers, and so on (see Appendix). The QE scale involves standards and expectations, focus on student achievement, faculty involvement and morale, and school spirit (see Appendix).

The top scorers on the QT scale were Isaac (91), National (86), Clark County (82), and Rosemead (80). Medium scorers were Washoe County (75), Mountain View (73), San Gabriel (73), and Fresno (73). Low scorers included Sunnyside (70), Franklin McKinley (61), and Balsz (58). We believe that Clark County's high rating may be an anomaly, the result of selection of nonrepresentative schools for the sample. As we explained in Chapter 2, Clark County was a case in which we did not choose the schools to be visited. Instead, the district chose two schools for us to visit that were new and appeared to educate mainly middle-class White children; we saw few minority or LEP students in these schools.

On the QE scale a similar ranking was seen. Isaac again was first at 95. National and Mountain View followed at 76. San Gabriel (73), Rosemead (72), Clark County (70), Washoe County (70), and Fresno (70) were in the middle. Franklin McKinley (64), Sunnyside (62), and Balsz (60) were again the lowest on the scale. Mountain View and San Gabriel were low-performing districts yet scored in the middle range on Quality of Education. It is likely that they were rated so highly because they are both small, caring communities.

In districts that responded proactively to changing demographics, teachers tended to use the following instructional strategies and approaches:

- Teaching basic and advanced skills through meaningful tasks.
- Encouraging active student participation.

- Validating multicultural values and practices.
- Making connections with students' experiences.
- Using a literature-based language-arts program.
- Using manipulatives, realia, and alternative modes to teach concepts.

When we visited schools in high-performing districts, it was clear that modern, up-to-date teaching strategies were being followed by a majority of teachers. In low-performing districts, we observed traditional teaching strategies. Instruction was generally teacher talk with an occasional spattering of innovative practices. The focus was on delivering instruction, imparting knowledge to students, and reiterating basic skills and rules.

In high-performing districts, we observed teachers using meaningful tasks such as group projects on a theme to engage students and teach them thinking skills. In the National School District, one school had chosen evolution, and various groups of students worked on projects related to that theme. One group, for example, made a time line, another created papier-mâché animals depicting evolution, and yet another wrote stories tracing historical development. In another school, teachers incorporated skills building (for example, computational skills) into enjoyable activities such as kite building or rocket launching.

In low-performing and stable districts, few innovative teaching strategies such as the ones described above were seen. However, a few of these districts did show traces of innovation and quality in their teaching of skills. These included Mountain View, Sunnyside, Washoe County, and Clark County.

High-performing districts had classes in which students were actively involved in learning rather than in passively listening to teacher talk. Teachers relied on experiences and theme-based approaches, keeping lecturing to a minimum. They encouraged students to ask questions and to challenge them, carrying on a true two-way dialogue between themselves and their students. In general, low-performing districts did not display so much active student participation, although we did observe isolated incidents of this.

In schools in high-performing districts, we saw teachers who were in touch with students' cultural values. Pictures, sentences, and posters referring to various ethnic groups' activities, holidays, or practices were evident in classes and on walls. In addition, schools often had regular night-time activities for parents and families that validated various cultures (e.g., Worldwide Potluck). However, a few stable and low-performing districts also carried on similar activities. Some teachers, especially in schools with high concentrations of Hispanic youth, made use of universal values such as cooperative and nurturing behavior. For example, older students would tutor younger ones, or better English speakers would help LEP students.

Some low-performing districts, notably Mountain View and Sunnyside, scored very high on the Quality of Multiculturalism scale and showed evidence of teacher validation of multicultural values and practices. Other stable or low-performing districts showed no evidence of this, however.

In high-performing districts, we observed that teachers used experiences and incidents in students' lives for class projects. For example, in one Los Angeles area district, students were asked to write about their feelings concerning the 1992 Los Angeles riots. In low-performing districts, we glimpsed such teaching only occasionally.

Consistently, high-performing districts tended to use a literature-based approach to language arts. In some cases, they also used a whole-language approach. Other districts were more likely to use traditional basal readers and phonics. Some stable and low performers, however, used a literature-based approach, including both Mountain View and Washoe County.

In high-performing districts, classrooms were likely to have plenty of materials for student use. These included math manipulatives, beads, and Cuisinaire rods. In addition, teachers tended to use manipulatives, realia, and alternative modes for teaching rather than resorting to the traditional "show and tell." Several teachers used songs and records in teaching language arts. In one classroom we visited, a teacher used measuring sticks and tapes to teach length, width, and area. In a classroom activity, the students measured lots of things, including their own heights.

In low-performing and stable districts, fewer manipulatives and realia were used. Materials were not as plentiful as in high positive-change districts. Mountain View, Clark County, and Sunnyside did show some examples of using manipulatives and realia, but they were not widespread.

## INSTRUCTIONAL QUALITY: ACCESS TO EDUCATIONAL PROGRAMS

In this section we focus on educational programs that may influence a district's outcomes. We begin by describing Chapter 1 and other compensatory programs and review the ideal components in a Chapter 1 program. Districts are compared and contrasted on the characteristics of their Chapter 1 programs. We then review the ideal components of a second-language program and describe bilingual and ESL programs. Districtwide commitments to second-language programs and effective instructional practices are highlighted. Newcomer programs that exist in several districts are also described. Districts are compared and contrasted on characteristics of their bilingual and ESL programs. Finally, we describe other educational programs such as tutoring and homework programs and once again compare and contrast the districts with regard to these.

## Chapter 1 Programs

The comparatively vast categorical program Title I (of the Elementary and Secondary Education Act of 1965) allocates funds through state agencies to local school districts with schools that host large numbers of disadvantaged children. The policy concept guiding Title I was that district educators would plan programs to deliver instruction and instructional support to low-income students in ways that would offset or "compensate" for their background deprivations.

No other intervention—federal, state, local, or private—comes near the financial magnitude and programmatic centrality of Title I in public schooling. Title I, superseded by Chapter 1 amendments in 1981, continues to invest federal funds in the goals of overcoming educational deprivation associated with poverty and racial/ethnic minority status and of improving learning opportunities for children in poverty. Chapter 1's funding level in 1996 exceeds $6 billion; the programs it supports locally are intended to serve 5 million schoolchildren, or 1 in every 9 children in the nation.

Many today believe that Chapter 1 and Head Start programs are generally beneficial but that the severity of the learning deficits of disadvantaged children is such that participation in Chapter 1 helps to raise their (very low) scores only slightly. In 1983, Mullin and Summers published a meta-analysis of 47 compensatory education programs that included Title I program evaluations. Their major findings were the following:

- The programs have a small positive effect on academic achievement of poor and low-achieving students.
- Most evaluations have faulty methodology and thus overstate cognitive outcomes.
- The fadeout phenomenon is characteristic, in that cognitive gains are greater in the early years, followed by a sharp decline.
- The programs are generally not cost-effective.
- No particular model or characteristic of a model is systematically related to its effectiveness.

Most school districts use their Chapter 1 funds to deliver heightened or enhanced instruction in the basic skill domains of elementary-level reading, writing, and mathematics. They also utilize the funds to provide classroom aides and resources teachers or to reduce class size or instructional group size. Given the magnitude of annual Chapter 1 investments, we use these programs as a starting point for our analysis of instructional delivery programs among our sampled districts.

In this study, all of the districts and most of the schools visited received Chapter 1 money and had some type of Chapter 1 program. Many of the Chapter 1 schools were so designated because they were located in high-poverty areas and more than 75% of their children qualified.

High-performing districts tended to use in-class, schoolwide, or after-school Chapter 1 programs to supplement and enrich the core curriculum. However, these uses of Chapter 1 funds were found in almost all of the sampled districts. Two of the high-performing districts (Isaac and Rose-mead) used either in-class or before- or after-school Chapter 1 "add-on" programs. Some districts conducted summer schools for enrichment with Chapter 1 funds. Although several of the low-performing districts (including Fresno, Clark County and Franklin McKinley) had Chapter 1 pull-out programs, some stable or low-performing districts used in-class or after-school Chapter 1 programs. Sunnyside, also a low-performing district, previously had a pull-out Chapter 1 program but changed to a before- and after-school program. Balsz, a stable district, recently changed from a pull-out to an in-class program.

In Chapter 1 schoolwide projects, the schools focused on children with special needs, but the curriculum was generally integrated (e.g., science and language arts). The Chapter 1 teacher planned cooperatively with grade-level teachers. For example, in the National School District, each school (in conjunction with parents) planned, implemented, and evaluated its Chapter 1 and School Improvement Plan program.

The Isaac School District also used the schoolwide mode. This allowed for school-site decision making regarding allocation of funds and resulted in greater coordination between classroom instruction and Chapter 1 program staff as well as increased parent involvement. The district held many parent workshops, offered GED classes, and published newsletters. The district developed an administrative guide to Chapter 1 and was attempting to increase the number of students eligible for Chapter 1.

## Second-Language Programs

Research has established that second-language learners require about 2 to 3 years to acquire basic proficiency in second-language skills (basic interpersonal communication skills, or BICS) and from 4 to 10 years to acquire sufficient cognitive-academic language proficiency skills (CALPS) to score at grade level in academic achievement in the second language (Collier, 1992; Krashen & Biber, 1988). Some variance exists in the time it takes to acquire basic proficiency, based on student characteristics such as prior schooling in the native language or facility in the second language. A great deal of variance exists in the time it takes LEP students to acquire grade-level cognitive-academic skills in the subject areas. Some of this variance can be attributed to the type of instructional programs given to second-language learners (Krashen & Biber, 1988).

**Types of ESL Programs and Models.** In classrooms, a wide variety of second-language programs and models operate. Many program models exist today, including English as a second language (ESL), transitional bilingual education, bilingual late and early exit, sheltered English, structured immersion, submersion, and transitional maintenance (Casteneda, 1992). These programs are often defined in terms of funding source (e.g., Title VII) (Merino, 1991). Many second-language programs provide some instruction in both languages, with a transition to English as soon as possible. Few programs use the primary language of the children served. Even in bilingual programs that use two languages, the percentage of time spent in English and that spent in the primary language vary a great deal (Ramirez et al., 1992).

It is evident that the presence of a second-language program does not guarantee high student achievement or "success." Models that rely on English for instruction (ESL and sheltered English) do not require teachers fluent in the students' native languages and are used primarily in schools serving a mixture of students from multiple-language groups. Although these approaches are sometimes necessary in multiple-language settings, they are not optimal. ESL is generally a pull-out model and results in discontinuities between the classroom teacher and the ESL pull-out teacher. The sheltered English approach sometimes incorporates low expectations and may involve an overly simplified curriculum (Berman et al., 1992).

Several demographic conditions influence the choice of programs or models for LEP students: whether these students all speak the same non-English language or whether they speak several, with no single language spoken by a large number of LEP students; the concentration of LEP students compared with that of other students in the district or school; and the stability of demographic conditions. It is easier for districts with large concentrations of one language group (in most cases, Spanish) to create bilingual programs.

Several bilingual models are used in schools. Although these are preferable to ESL and other similar approaches because they develop the native language skills of LEP students and thus enable them to build a foundation for language development, they generally can be used only when the situation offers a concentration of one single non-English-language group and a sufficient number of teachers fluent in that language.

Many reviews of bilingual education programs report mixed results. Some show small but positive effects (Merino, 1991). Few studies have actually included observational data on program implementation in the classroom, but the practice is becoming more frequent.

On the basis of a statewide evaluation of bilingual education models in California, Berman et al. (1992) concluded that comparable student outcome data by which to judge one bilingual education model versus others do not exist. Thus research cannot currently identify which approach is the most effective. Berman et al. also concluded that, rather than asking which bilingual model is superior, districts and schools should identify conditions under which one or a combination of approaches is best suited and adapt the model to match their circumstances. For example, the ESL pull-out approach can be combined with the use of native-speaking aides in the main classroom who work with LEP children in small groups. In addition, Berman et al. identified three crucial factors that affect the implementation of any second-language program: (a) a shared vision and sensitivity to LEP students' cultural heritage; (b) suitable staff, ongoing training, and resource allocation; and (c) collaborative coordination and articulation between elementary and secondary schools.

**Effective Instruction in Second-Language Programs.** Garcia (1992) reviewed research studies that documented effective instructional practices used with linguistically and culturally diverse students. Several descriptive studies identified specific schools whose language minority students were successful academically, with academic achievement at or above national averages. Eight common attributes were identified in the instructional organization of the classrooms studied:

1. High level of verbal communication between teacher and students, and among students.
2. Integration of basic skills instruction with instruction in other subjects.
3. Organization of instruction around themes.
4. Use of collaborative learning groups.
5. Students allowed to progress naturally and without pressure from writing in their native language to writing later in English.
6. Highly committed teachers who act as student advocates.
7. Principal support for teachers.
8. Parents active in school activities.

Garcia further notes that the greater the number of language groups present, the greater the need for academic content closely related to the child's own environment and experience. Academic skills in the content areas can be applied through hands-on interactive activities that allow students to explore issues of significance in their lives, such as investigating the quality of the local water supply. Garcia also feels that we should integrate the curriculum. This means that multiple content areas such as math and social studies and language-learning activities should be centered around a theme. Children should be offered opportunities to study topics in depth. It is important to note that the eight attributes identified (with the exception of the fifth) are practices that can be considered effective for all children, not just LEP students.

The components of an ideal instructional delivery system in the area of second-language programs include a comprehensive bilingual program in schools that have a large concentration of one language group, an ESL or sheltered English program for schools with more than one dominant language group, the availability of primary-language materials, a sufficient number of bilingual teachers and aides, a staff knowledgeable about bilingual and multicultural issues, the integration of English language development with content area instruction, and a process through which students can progress naturally from writing in their primary language to writing later in English. (See Figure 3.1.)

**A Commitment to Educate Language Minority Students.** We found that high-performing districts had a strong policy commitment to educate language minority students and to provide teachers with the supportive context they needed to deliver quality instruction to students. Overall, the high-performing districts illustrate several important manifestations of strong district-level commitment: (a) allocation of monetary resources; (b) long-term institutional commitment; and (c) program flexibility to modify services as the language and instructional needs of students change over time.

A strong commitment to meeting language minority students' needs was manifested in the National and Rosemead districts through bilingual programs in place for more than 20 years. In both cases the programs operated under school board-sanctioned master plans that set goals and objectives but also established as a basic premise the need for the programs to evolve over time to respond to changing demographics.

Rosemead provides an excellent example of such program evolution. Changes in the bilingual program took place gradually, moving from providing bilingual services to Spanish-speaking students to increasingly using sheltered instructional and ESL techniques to address the needs of a multilingual student population. In 1980, the bilingual program was restricted to kindergarten. In 1984, the district hired a full-time ESL teacher for every school, and it continues to increase the number of bilingual/ESL teachers and paraprofessionals.

In Isaac, during the past decade, funds allocated to the purpose of bilingual education increased by over 650%. Bilingual education is now the centerpiece of Isaac's instructional program, and bilingual classes are offered at all schools. Programs for Spanish-speaking students and their parents also permeate the district. After visiting classrooms and talking to teachers, administrators, parents, and students, our site-visit team concluded that meeting the needs of LEP students and their families was the raison d'être of the district, so focused are its energies.

When this kind of district-level commitment was absent, teachers stressed the negative impact on education. For example, in Fresno the consensus among teachers was that the district had never supported bilingual education. Consequently, they felt it would never become a viable alternative for large segments of the student population who speak a common language, such as Spanish. In fact, over time Fresno's initial interest in bilingual education dwindled to the point that it now uses primarily ESL pull-out programs at the elementary level.

The teachers we interviewed in Fresno agreed that if a bilingual program received financial and policy support from the district, such a program would meet the needs of many children who presently receive ESL instruction for limited periods during the day and limited primary-language support. Similarly, several individuals in the district commented that lack of a strong commitment also meant limited emphasis on recruiting bilingual teachers, teachers with diverse cultural backgrounds, or paraprofessionals who could provide students with primary-language support. There was also a concern that the needs of newcomer and LEP students at the high school level were ignored and that, as a consequence, many were illiterate in both English and their first language (most often Spanish).

The presence of districtwide programs also had strong positive effects in low-performing districts. For example, Sunnyside administrators and teachers reported that the district was able to attract bilingual teachers because of its bilingual education program's strong reputation. In addition, they reported the program was a drawing card for recent immigrants from Mexico who, in part, settled in the district because it provides extensive bilingual services at all grade levels.

Stable districts provide examples of both stagnation and increasing commitment to programs for language minority students. With respect to the first dynamic, Franklin McKinley's bilingual and multicultural programs resemble those of 15 or 20 years ago, when issues of non- and limited-English-proficient students were first being addressed. Lack of a districtwide focus resulted in the absence of bilingual, intensive language, newcomer, or native-language literacy programs. Because of the extremely limited number of bilingual teachers, and a limited number of ESL teachers, instruction for LEP students was on a pull-out basis with tutorial services provided by native-language aides (when they were available).

By contrast, the Balsz School District has served a large minority population as long as anyone could remember, but because language minority students tended to be concentrated in a few schools until recently, the district is only now turning its attention to bilingual, ESL, and other linguistic and multicultural issues. Currently, pull-out ESL programs are the only programmatic treatment for LEP students, but this occurs in a context where Chapter 1 and special education are no longer pull-out programs. Consequently, there is widespread recognition that the program provided LEP students is a partial measure and that more effective instructional approaches need to be developed. This is also the sentiment in Clark County, where teachers felt they needed additional support from the district to respond effectively to the growing numbers of LEP Hispanic students. The district used ESL pull-out programs almost exclusively. As a result, most language minority students spent most of the day with an English-speaking teacher limited in the skills and knowledge to meet their needs. And in Clark County, as in all the districts, teachers told us how important effective staff development was for equipping them to deal effectively with changing student demographics.

High-performing districts were more likely to have a large, well-established bilingual education program and to use the students' primary language to build comprehension (e.g., Isaac, National, and Rosemead). With the exception of Mountain View (which had a large bilingual education program), low-performing districts tended to have ESL programs rather than bilingual programs or, in some cases, had only sheltered English classes.

Some of the districts visited had some sort of bilingual plan or master plan for language development, usually created in the 1980s. These ranged from very sketchy and basic to extremely well developed and comprehensive. Some included lesson plans and themes. The National School District (a high-performing district) developed their own Bilingual Education Master Plan, which outlines empirical and other bases for bilingual reform, the board's policy, characteristics of the program, program options, management procedures, identification procedures, procedures for transitioning, program planning, and content area information. The mission of the program is to develop cognitive academic language proficiency (CALP) in

English through use of students' primary language within a bilingual/ multicultural framework. Spanish-speaking children are instructed primarily in Spanish in K–3 to help them develop basic skills and to facilitate transition to English instruction in grades 4–6. The district has developed a team-teaching approach called Triad (a bilingual cooperative teacher model), a comprehensive procedure for placement of LEP students, and an oral development checklist by grade level. It also developed a "LAS Testing and Reclassification Handbook" that details the testing and classification procedures and processes.

Another example of a comprehensive bilingual education plan was Isaac's "Handbook," which includes a mission statement, purposes, legal mandates, a description of the transitional bilingual and ESL programs, an outline of research on second-language acquisition, teaching guidelines, information on effective teaching methods, procedures for assessment and classification, bilingual program job descriptions, and future strategies. In the future, modifications will be made to the program to include multicultural curriculum components, sheltered English, cooperative learning, and team teaching and to provide additional in-service training on language acquisition, second-language teaching strategies, and student assessment. Stipulations will also be made for additional parental involvement.

High-performing districts were more likely than others to provide primary-language materials both in classrooms and in libraries. Qualified teachers were observed using primary language and English and alternating between the two. Students were encouraged to use their primary language both in class and on the playground. They were allowed to progress naturally from writing in their primary language to writing in English later. Generally, high-performing districts used a whole-language, literature-based approach to language. Successful districts tended to have a more established bilingual education program and stricter, more elaborate criteria for transitioning students into English-only classes.

A majority of districts used some version of ESL. In general, ESL operates as a pull-out program, with a few exceptions. ESL pull-out was the most commonly used approach with Asian students. In Isaac, however, the small percentage of Asians in the district (1%) were taught in regular English-only classrooms rather than in an ESL program. The National School District had a relatively large proportion of Filipinos (13%) who were taught in sheltered English classes (according to the wishes of their parents). In Rosemead, Asian students (30% of the district's students) were not taught in bilingual classes, because of a lack of Vietnamese, Cantonese, and Mandarin teachers. Asian parents in Rosemead (and in several other districts) generally wanted their children to be taught in English. Some sheltered English and ESL classes were offered to the Asian students in Rosemead, and the district provided some bilingual aides. Several low-performing districts (Fresno, Mountain View, and Sunnyside) made very few provisions for Asian students. In Fresno, the need was particularly pressing, because Asians were 21% of the district population. Fresno used primarily ESL pull-out, with a few bilingual classes.

During a visit to an elementary school in a low-performing district, we viewed an ESL pull-out group being "instructed" in various words and sounds. The ESL teacher wrote words and phrases on the board and asked students to write the English words down. As the students worked, I (Hafner) approached one Hispanic boy and asked (in Spanish), "What are you doing?" He responded, "Copying letters from the board." I asked if he could read or understand them; he smiled and said no, and continued copying them.

Most of the schools visited (including those in high-, stable, and low-performing districts) used bilingual aides in the classrooms as tutors. In some cases, aides would conduct small reading groups, but, more commonly, they used one-on-one tutoring in the native language. However, the amount of time that each child received was very short (in all schools, an average of 20 to 30 minutes a day).

**Assessment Centers and Newcomer Programs.** Most districts had an explicit process by which students were tested in their native language, in many cases with the Language Assessment Scales (LAS). The degree to which information about these new students was passed on to their teachers, however, varied greatly. In many cases, teachers got almost no information and needed to guess the reading and literacy level of their students. Reclassification procedures (moving a student from a Spanish bilingual to an English program) varied greatly from district to district. In high-performing districts, criteria for transitioning were stricter than in other districts (e.g., students were kept in primary-language instruction as long as possible).

The National School District, Washoe County, and a few other districts had some version of a Needs Assessment Center or intake center, in which newcomers to the country or LEP students new to the district were screened, diagnosed, and placed. The center at National was very comprehensive and used a Bilingual Education Manual and Classification Manual.

National created a Needs Assessment Center in 1982 to quickly screen, diagnose, and place children new to the district. This center also identifies Chapter 1 students and determines and facilitates their most appropriate placement. A wide battery of assessments is used at the center. Testing results in a complete profile of a new student's abilities. Thus, when a new student begins school, the teacher knows the student's strengths and weaknesses and can better meet the child's individual needs.

Fresno had the largest and most comprehensive newcomer program of the districts visited. Serving about 600 students a year, it takes in recent immigrants in grades 7–12 for a one-semester program. It offers basic English-speaking skills, introduction to American culture, and ESL instruction in oral language, reading, math, world cultures, and life skills. It is funded through district and Title VII monies. Although staff are very dedicated and believe the program helps the newcomers, the program is widely criticized for being too short to prepare students fully for all-English instruction in regular high schools. There are so many newcomers that the district is forced to push the students out after a brief stay (usually 8 to 12 weeks). Indeed, we saw one result of this in the Fresno high school visited, where a large number of newcomer students in certain remedial classes were at a very low literacy level in English and were not able to comprehend much of what the teachers said.

The Isaac School District has a program for newcomers called High Intensity Language Training (HILT). It operates in two ways. In one school, it consists of two 1.5-hour sessions a week held before and after school. At other schools, it is a full-time program, lasting for 2 to 3 years, of intensive training in native-language skills before students are transitioned into English.

In Washoe County, new students could stay at the intake centers for 6 to 12 weeks and were usually taught in sheltered classes. Most Washoe County students were pushed out into regular schools and classes after 2 months and did not have even rudimentary English skills.

Overall, in this study, several programmatic and instructional features were found to be effective in multiple-language settings. High-performing districts displayed some unique characteristics that included placing a high priority on hiring bilingual teachers and aides, providing primary-language materials and support, encouraging students to use their primary language, and employing the whole-language approach (among others). In general, the main instructional goal in these districts was student language development, and efforts were focused on providing equal opportunities for all students to learn English.

## Other Educational Programs

Many other educational programs were evident in the sampled schools, including a multitude devoted to academics, health, and family. Only the academic programs are discussed in this chapter; the others are discussed in Chapter 6. Most of the LEAs had numerous academic programs designed to meet the needs of newcomer and educationally disadvantaged students.

Many of the schools visited (including many elementary schools) had computer labs, in both high-performing and low-performing districts. Only a few teachers in elementary schools had their own computers in their classrooms. Most commonly, classes of students were pulled out to attend computer lab once a week. The children would spend 30 to 45 minutes in the lab, working on writing, math skills, or word-processing skills (depending on students' age level). The National School District had one elementary school with an extensive computer lab, and in this school, students used the lab 25 minutes each day. In the San Gabriel and Franklin McKinley districts, students used the lab once a week. No exemplary computer programs were evident.

Personalized programs are individualized and usually designed for at-risk students. They are often independent study classes offered so students can go at their own pace. They appeared to be somewhat remedial in nature. Some high-performing, low-performing, and stable districts had personalized or individualized programs.

Many schools offered after-school homework programs to provide academic and cultural enrichment to children. High-performing districts were no more likely than other districts to have this type of program.

Some districts offered parent education workshops on how to help one's child with homework. These were considered especially useful for non-English-speaking and low-literacy-level parents. High-performing districts were no more likely than other districts to have this type of program.

In general, teachers in classrooms seemed to focus on writing and to spend a lot of classroom time writing. Many of the districts and schools in the study had participated in area writing projects, such as the California Writing Project or the California Literature Project. In addition, some districts sponsored student writing contests with prizes. Although some low-performing districts participated in such projects, high-performing districts were more likely to do so.

Some preschool programs were offered in the districts visited. However, high-performing districts did not seem to be more likely than other districts to have this type of program. Some examples include the TYKE pre-K at-risk program in San Gabriel and a preschool program for 4-year-old at-risk children at two schools in Franklin McKinley. National had a child development center for at-risk children aged 3 to 8 that provided an enriched environment to enhance students' social, cognitive, and physical development. National also provided an extended day kindergarten with an extra 1.5 hours a day of language development. Rosemead had a program called Early Prevention of School Failure for 4- to 7-year-olds.

Sunnyside had a districtwide preschool program. Isaac established a non-graded primary school 2 years ago, for grades K–3.

Many of the districts visited had math competitions, field days, and prizes. High-performing districts in some cases appeared to have more comprehensive programs. For example, Rosemead had a family math program, a Spanish math program, and frequent math contests.

Many programs for at-risk children existed in the districts in all three performance categories. One district with a plethora of at-risk programs was Isaac, which listed at least 36 separate programs in one of its publications. They ranged from a full-day kindergarten and preschool library to elementary counseling and a latchkey program; from "say no to drugs" and after-school homework to a mental health team and peer counseling. This district had a program for immigrant education as well as Title VII, Chapter 1, Even Start, Bright Start, and DARE programs.

Sunnyside and San Gabriel (both low-performing districts) were the only districts identified as using the Reading Recovery program. This extensive reading program includes one-on-one tutoring.

The modified curriculum program is a watered-down version of the regular curriculum for low-ability children. Balsz used it, and Washoe County used something similar called alternative education classes. Neither is generally considered desirable, because both are remedial and deny students access to the core curriculum. This type of program was not widely used.

Many districts in the sample had gifted and talented (GATE) programs and classes. It appeared, however, that high-performing districts did not put much emphasis on GATE and focused rather on "all children can learn" and on high expectations for all.

## CONCLUSIONS

Table 3.2 displays the extent to which sample districts (arranged in order from high-performing to low-performing) show elements or components of an ideal instructional delivery system. The elements should not be seen as all-or-nothing but as a type of continuum. Although the top three high-performing districts showed all the elements of an ideal instructional delivery system, some stable or low-performing districts showed one or more. It is obvious that no one district can fulfill the ideal perfectly but some come close. These are districts that have shown widespread changes in their organization, curriculum, and instruction.

In addition, Table 3.2 lists the overall rank of the districts on the five scale scores. Isaac, National, and Rosemead, as expected, scored in the top

**Table 3.2 Districts Showing Elements/Components of an Ideal Instructional Delivery System**

| District | Teacher Quality | Instructional Organizational Structures | Standards and Assessments | Instructional Quality: Strategies | Optimal 2nd Language Programs | Optimal Chapter 1 Programs | Overall Rank Scale Scores |
|---|---|---|---|---|---|---|---|
| Isaac | ++ | ++ | ++ | ++ | ++ | ++ | 1 |
| Rosemead | ++ | ++ | + | ++ | ++ | ++ | 4 |
| National | ++ | ++ | ++ | ++ | ++ | ++ | 2 |
| Franklin | | | | | | | 10 |
| Washoe | | | | + | | | 8 |
| Clark Co | | | | + | | | 7 |
| Balsz | + | + | | | | | 11 |
| SanGabriel | | + | | | + | + | 6 |
| Fresno | | | | | | | 5 |
| Sunnyside | + | | + | + | ++ | + | 9 |
| Mt.View | + | | | + | + | | 3 |

*Key:* + = some elements     ++ = many or most elements

four. Surprisingly, Mountain View scored third overall, mainly because of its high ratings on QM, QI, and QE scales. Washoe County and Clark County ranked in the middle range, as did Fresno and San Gabriel. The bottom scorers were Sunnyside (a low performer), Franklin McKinley, and Balsz (stable performers). We discussed earlier the possible reasons for these anomalies.

In the area of teacher characteristics and teacher quality, high-performing districts were more likely than others to show effective staff development programs and to have more teachers with ethnic-linguistic profiles similar to those of their students. In addition, teachers had more positive attitudes, higher morale, and were more likely to hold high expectations of students.

In the area of instructional organization, cooperative learning was used by a majority of districts. In high-performing districts, team teaching and teacher collaboration were common, especially in primary grades in large blocks of time. Grade-level and content-area articulation were evident, as well as a high level of teacher communication. Peer and cross-age tutoring and mentoring were common. Combination (multi-age) classes and heterogeneous grouping were seen in most high positive-change districts. More important, all students, whether LEP or not, low ability or high, had access to a rich common core curriculum.

In the area of objectives, standards, and assessment, some of the characteristics of the high-performing districts included a focus on students and their outcomes, high expectations, use of authentic classroom assessments such as portfolios, and a shared vision of instructional goals. A capacity-building model, rather than a deficit model, was evident. Low-performing districts conducted business as usual, lecturing and using worksheets, and focusing on skill building and drills. They tended to use traditional achievement tests, and very little innovation was observed.

In the area of instructional quality, a marked difference was seen between high-performing and low-performing districts. However, some stable or low-performing districts showed one or more elements of the ideal system. In high-performing districts, teachers tended to use meaning-centered strategies and to encourage active student participation. Basic and advanced tasks were taught through meaningful projects and themes. The whole-language approach was common. Teachers integrated content area frameworks with their instruction.

In the area of second-language programs, several practices and programmatic and instructional features were found to be effective in multiple-language settings. High-performing districts tended to provide comprehensive programs and resources and to serve many of their LEP students; to place high priority on hiring bilingual teachers; to provide sufficient primary-language materials; to encourage students to use their primary language; to allow students to progress naturally from writing in their native language to writing in English; to use a whole-language, literature-based approach to language; to use stricter, more elaborate criteria for transitioning students; to have a needs assessment or newcomer center; and to provide sheltered content classes to smaller language groups. By contrast, low-performing districts had fewer bilingual teachers; had some bilingual aides for short periods; used ESL pull-out; served very few bilingual students; and made few provisions for Asian students.

With regard to academic programs, high-performing districts were more likely to participate in writing projects such as the California Writing Project. In addition, they were more likely to have comprehensive mathematics programs, including math competitions, family math, and field days. They were also less likely to place an emphasis on the gifted and talented and to focus more on "all children can learn," with high expectations for all.

Low-performing districts tended to show one of two patterns. In one, districts had many traditional categorical programs such as special education, gifted and talented, after-school tutoring, latchkey programs, and so forth. In the other, showing a "project mentality," districts took sporadic and short-lived leaps into various innovative programs or practices (e.g., Reading Recovery or outcomes-based education). They did not, however, show a concerted systemic approach to school improvement over a period of time.

In the area of Chapter 1 and other programs for the disadvantaged, all of the sample districts had Chapter 1 programs, and many of the schools were designated as Chapter 1 schools. High-performing districts tended to use in-class, schoolwide, or after-school programs. Although several of the other districts had Chapter 1 pull-out programs, a few districts also used in-class or after-school programs. There was an emerging trend toward using schoolwide, in-class, or after-school programs and toward using Chapter 1 monies to supplement and enrich the core curriculum.

Most of the LEAs had numerous programs designed to meet the needs of newcomers and educationally disadvantaged students. If one examines the "other" educational programs available in sample districts, it is evident that the existence of special programs bore little relationship to the success of a district in serving educationally disadvantaged students and newcomers (with a couple of exceptions).

Overall, in order to distill down the many aspects of staff, instruction, and programs that have been presented, it is necessary to ask: What counts most? Which aspects are essential in ensuring a quality educational experience for students? It may be possible to identify a set of critical elements that can make or break a district's efforts.

Essential aspects of a quality school system appear to be the following:

- A strong focus on teacher quality and comprehensive staff development and rewards for professional development.
- A focus on teacher collaboration, planning, and decision making.
- Instructional organizational structures that provide opportunities for teachers to work together and enable them to deliver effective instruction (team teaching, use of flexible grouping methods, time for teacher meetings).

In addition, high-performing districts have comprehensive second-language programs and resources and provide sufficient primary-language materials. Often, they also have newcomer centers or classes and provide sheltered content classes to small language groups. Whether all of these individual factors are necessary in order for a district to be effective is a question not easily answered, although it appears that our high-achieving districts did have all of these pieces in place.

The picture that emerges of districts' teaching staffs and instructional programs is complex and defies simple categorizations or sweeping generalizations. As we have mentioned, there were exceptions to most trends we observed. In some cases, low-performing districts had far higher percentages of minority and bilingual teachers than did high-performing districts. These included staffs composed largely of minority teachers who were recruited before the dramatic shift in student demographics the districts experienced, as well as minority teachers hired to cope specifically with those shifts. Some low-performing districts operated bilingual programs that were considered exemplary and an advantage when recruiting teachers. Some of the low-performing and stable districts showed elements of an ideal instructional delivery system. Still, the high-performing districts could be differentiated from the low-performing districts by their efforts on a number of related fronts.

# 4

# Community History and Culture

In order to answer the study's research questions regarding organizational and cultural correlates of models of good practice, we focused our sights on local community history and cultural aspects that appeared to be significant contributors. We reasoned that these factors were important variables in light of the pervasive stratification that persists and acts to structure inequality of results for low SES students. We see the degree of intensity of social structural dominance as being shaped in part by local history and political and social cultures. Although we know that structural dominance applies to mainstream groups, it is unclear whether the concept also applies in the recent situation of swift demographic changes in numbers of language and ethnic minority newcomers.

This chapter describes the community history of high-performing versus stable or low-performing districts, local cultural and political factors that exist in various types of districts, and distinctive community structural features—such as social integration, size, and expenditures—that differentiate between district success and failure. It identifies the characteristics of districts that are intentionally moving to countervail the strong effects of structural dominance. And it contrasts two distinct types of district settings: those that are proactive and fluidly adaptive and those that are reactive and change-resistant.

## HISTORY

In marked contrast to school districts in other geographical regions of the United States, those we studied in the Western region all have chronologically short histories. They are reasonably old for the Far West, but they are very young when compared with those in the nation's Northeastern and Southern regions. A few of the communities reach back to the Spanish mission era, and all of them were established between 1860 and 1900. They took their current demographic and economic forms only after 1950, however.

California's population increased sixfold in the last 40 years, while Arizona and Nevada grew to roughly three times their pre–World War II population size. So, like the ones we selected to study, the communities within these states generally are creations of the postwar period.

Moreover, between 1900 and 1950, our sample communities were uniformly rural, not urban or suburban. Ten of the eleven were agricultural trade centers in their earlier formative periods. They comprised farm villages, ranches, groves, and vineyard settlements. The eleventh, Sunnyside, on the far fringe of Tucson, was a copper mineworkers' settlement from its beginnings until 1984, when the mines were closed.

The transition of these communities from rural villages into edge cities and suburbs took place during World War II for some districts—Isaac in Phoenix, Arizona, for instance. In contrast, Franklin McKinley near San Jose, California, changed from an area of 50 vineyards and ranches into a part of Silicon Valley only in the 1960s.

## High-Performing Districts

What a district's historic economic function and work-force composition was and how long ago its transition toward metropolitanization began offer clues to the performance of its schools. Among our three high-performing districts, Isaac changed after 1975 from an enrollment that was 75% Anglo to one that is 72% Hispanic. Up until then, minority students came from families who had been settled in Isaac for two or more generations. After 1975, half of the students entering as newcomers were new not only to Isaac but also to the United States.

Isaac's economy also changed rapidly. During World War II it became the site for a large aluminum factory geared to produce military materials. By 1950, its agrarian legacy was nearly dead. By 1970, its long-established households began to move away and the wartime housing— by then dilapidated and cheap—became home to successive waves of Mexican and Latino families migrating to Arizona in search of new lives.

Just a few miles north of the Mexican border, the National School District in California reaches back to the time when it was a Spanish mission. Many Filipino and Hispanic families have lived there since 1940, when National provided housing for U.S. Navy personnel based in nearby San Diego. After World War II, the community grew slowly from 1950 into the 1970s. Between 1980 and 1984, however, this once stable and small exurban settlement became one of the fastest-growing communities in the nation. As hundreds of newly arriving Filipino and Latino families settled in National City, the National School District began hosting three times as many NEP and LEP children as they had in 1979.

Rosemead, in the Los Angeles area, is another district founded as a rural, agricultural community in the mid-1800s, and it continued as such until the 1960s. Mainly because of the high number of immigrant Southeast Asian and Mexican families settling there between 1970 and 1990, however, Rosemead reversed its enrollment composition from 96% Anglo to only 16%. By the late 1980s, it was just another edge city with such an area's attendant problems. Here, the Asian population grew from 2% to 34%, and the number of Asians and Hispanics swelled from 0.5% to 50% during the same period. In other words, Rosemead underwent very swift demographic and multi-ethnic change, and most of that change took place during the 1980s. Indeed, this district had to expand its public schools so quickly that about 44% of its current teachers were hired between 1987 and 1991.

## Districts with Little or No Change

As we noted above, Franklin McKinley, on the edge of San Jose, California, remained essentially rural into the 1960s, with cattle ranches and vineyards the basis of its economy. Then it was overtaken by the urban sprawl of Silicon Valley. It had always hosted LEP students, nearly all of them Hispanic. But late in the 1970s, Franklin McKinley also became the settlement for thousands of Vietnamese families, and, in more recent years, for additional hundreds of impoverished Cambodians.

Between 1986 and 1992, Franklin McKinley became a kind of dormitory suburb for working-class households whose wage earners work primarily in service industries in the Bay Area, some working in Silicon Valley computer manufacturing plants that have not yet been relocated overseas. Thus, by the mid-1980s, its student ethnic composition was 53% Hispanic and 28% Asian, including mainly Vietnamese and Cambodian youngsters.

Among the other districts with little change in achievement outcomes is Washoe County, Nevada. In contrast to the three high-performing districts, Washoe began its urbanization in the 1930s, when nearby Reno emerged as a divorce mill and gambling nexus for the nation. It grew tremendously in the 1960s and then added 40% more students between 1980 and 1990. For all of this growth in numbers, however, Washoe County never achieved a large ethnic composition. More than 90% of its students were Anglos in 1960, 89% in 1980, and 79% in 1990. Its largest minority is Hispanic, at 11% of the population. Its profoundly and pervasively Anglo middle-class population and correlative political culture thus changed very little during the period of its greatest enrollment increase.

Clark County, Nevada, offers a similar story. Located around Las Vegas, the county experienced enormous population growth during the 1980s; the district added 70 new school buildings during that one decade. Yet it remained 68% Anglo in 1992. The number of Hispanic and Black students increased slightly over time. However, minority students' poverty and their racial isolation persisted during the 1980 to 1990 period of overall growth.

## Low-Performing Districts

Like our high-performing districts, some of the low-performing districts also underwent changes but of a different kind. These districts have traditionally had large numbers of ethnic minorities. San Gabriel, the city that the San Gabriel School District serves, for instance, is a community that has been run by wealthy, politically conservative Anglos for 50 years. Hispanics have comprised two thirds to four fifths of all households for several decades but have not been integrated socially into the community. Rather, they have tended to be ethnically isolated in the immediate vicinity of one school, the district's oldest facility, which itself is very near the original site of the Spanish mission. During the 1980s, however, many of the multigeneration, middle-class Hispanic households moved away from San Gabriel and were succeeded by low-income, newcoming immigrant Latinos and Vietnamese. Thus San Gabriel has been comprised of two major ethnic groups for several generations, yet it has been segregated ethnically and dominated in all respects by Anglos. As the long-established yet ghettoized Hispanics have been replaced since 1980 by Latino and Vietnamese newcomers, the old patterns have prevailed even while the historic Hispanic middle class has disappeared.

Balsz, near Phoenix, is another low performer in which the long-standing Hispanic settlers moved out during the 1980s to be replaced by new Latinos. Fresno, located in the Central Valley of California, began as a rural agricultural trading center; indeed, Fresno has maintained that original function and is to this day surrounded by large farms. It has had a high number of migrant and seasonal fruit and vegetable workers and their families for over 50 years.

The major change Fresno experienced in the 1980s was explosive overall population growth. Between 1980 and 1990, it became the third largest public school district in California. Fresno had always accommodated a large Hispanic population, but in the 1980s it added a burgeoning Asian and Southeast Asian population.

Sunnyside is another low performer with a history that differs fundamentally from that of the high-gain districts. From its initial formation, Sunnyside was a kind of fringe barrio for Tucson's Hispanic households.

Most of them were attached to the copper-mining industry, but some also chose to live there because housing was cheap and because there was a kind of built-in scheme of ethnic isolation. Two deep changes took place during the 1980s: The native Arizonan Hispanic families began to move away as the mines shut down, and these families were replaced by Mexican and Central American newcomers who were economically poorer, less well educated, and culturally unassimilated.

The city that subsumes the Mountain View School District also differs from our high-performing communities. As one of the first North American settlements in southern California, it is older than any of our other sample communities. Indeed, it has been a city for nearly all of this century. Like Isaac, National, and Rosemead, Mountain View came to be absorbed into the surrounding metropolitan area. Los Angeles transformed its real estate and made it into a small edge city during the 1960s, ending its earlier rural character. Industrial and commercial land values soared, while older housing came under new pressure to serve lower income households in search of some affordable shelter in a region of skyrocketing prices. Thus the numbers of immigrant Mexican and Central American households swelled, and the number of Asian, principally Taiwanese, households doubled during the 1980s. Hispanic students had predominated in Mountain View for several generations, but the older, more native families moved away after 1980 and were replaced by lower income newcomers while population totals soared.

## Implications

Historical review thus suggests that ethnic and language minority children were best served in the three communities that changed most completely and dramatically from rural and predominantly Anglo settlements to metropolitan and very predominantly minority settlements within the past 15 years. A fourth community, Franklin McKinley, paralleled this pattern closely. Low-performing districts have had long histories of hosting large percentages of minority group members.

## LOCAL CULTURE

Every American public school district functions within a local cultural context. As Corbett and Rossman (1988) note,

Culture describes the way things are. It provides the contextual clues necessary to interpret events, behaviors, words, and acts—and gives them meaning. Culture also prescribes the ways in which people should act, regulating appropriate and acceptable behaviors in given situations. (p. 37)

There are some national cultural features that permeate public schools, creating a few uniformities that facilitate the movement of staff and students from region to region without baffling estrangement. There are also important regional and state features, especially those features of political culture that shape educational power relations, governance arrangements, and levels of funding.

Tropman (1977) enumerates the ways in which both state and local cultures are shaped by political value preferences along a series of enduring-value dimensions. For example, school districts vary greatly in the extent to which their boards, superintendents, and staff have what Tropman calls a collective, public-regarding value preference, as distinguished from a privatistic, private-regarding preference. On this dimension of local culture, the public regarding end point characterizes communities in which marked help, voluntarism, philanthropy, and widespread involvement in social control are sources of pride. The private-regarding end point characterizes communities that stress self-reliance, a focus on the private lives of households and individuals, and a low level of involvement in social-control efforts.

In this study, our main concern, like the daily life concerns of the people who work in the districts, was with the cultures of local communities and districts. These have a certain crucial significance because districts, and the oldest schools within them, were the first educational service providers and continue to have substantial operating autonomy.

## High-Performing Districts

The Isaac School District operates within the context of Maricopa County and the City of Phoenix. That context is extremely segmented, with 53 separate and independent districts operating within the county and the city combined. This circumstance was commonplace in American education until 1950. District consolidations brought the number of separate districts nationwide down between 1940 and 1970 from more than 100,000 to fewer than 16,000. But Arizona, with its soaring population growth over the same period, remained organized in the pre-1940 tradition. Arizona's political culture has been quite consistent throughout the century: independent, laissez-faire, and competitively separatistic rather than collaborative and unifying (Sacken & Medina, 1990).

Isaac is one of the oldest school districts in Arizona. Yet it has "gone it alone" in the midst of tremendous urbanization from its rural beginnings in 1876 to the present day. Isaac has a "do it yourself" political culture. Mormon farmers created it, and one of them, the first superintendent, ran the district and its schools like a ranch for the first half of the 20th century. The Isaac culture was nurtured by the Mormon tradition, which stresses frugality and initiative. Isaac became expert at securing federal funds during the World War II years, when war industries gave it a military impact status. It maintained this advantage painstakingly into the 1970s. Today it generates more than 14% of its operating budget from entrepreneurial efforts to seek out and win federal contract and grant awards.

Originally, under the Mormons, Isaac developed a cultural tradition of intramural cooperation and harmony, combined with strong competitiveness in varsity athletic contests with other schools. When the population shifted after 1975 from Anglo to Hispanic (with most Mormons leaving the area), the organizing patterns of the Mormons prevailed and persisted at the same time they accommodated the cultural contributions of the newcomers.

The familialism of the Mexican tradition became incorporated strongly into almost every activity pursued by the people of Isaac. Although Isaac is situated within a sprawling tangle of warehouses and light industries, and though it is shredded by a large interstate highway and several miles of rail yards, the district functions much like a self-contained community of interest. Its families know one another within the school subdistricts and even across the district at the junior high school level. Its school administrators and staff behave as if they are social intimates, even though many individuals are young and have only recently arrived. And the school board members and senior administrators are widely and well known and esteemed, and trust and warm social sentiments are the lubricants of school and community alike.

Today Isaac is culturally unified around its predominantly Hispanic heritage. Yet the inclusiveness of this heritage makes other groups and their customs equally welcome and respected. It takes its tradition of frugality and prudence from its roots in the desert farming tradition, and it is invigorated by pitting itself competitively and programmatically against the county and state, which are perceived by Isaac leaders as both Anglo and indifferent to Hispanics.

The political culture of the National School District evolved from the community's origins as a residential adjunct to the San Diego naval base, and this legacy continues to this day. This is a culture in which Anglo values and customs have long dominated. The U.S. Navy changed substantially during the 1970s and 1980s, however, becoming more equitable socially, opening itself to women on ships and in the air, and desegregating its leadership ranks ethnically. From its beginning until now, moreover, the close association with navy families has meant for the National School District a tradition of public-regarding service.

National has built upon its foundation in naval tradition and, since 1970, has increased its value preference for equality. Until a decade ago, Anglos predominated on the school board and in the senior administration. The school board has recently diversified its membership, however, to include three minority members out of eight. Teachers and other professional staff have turned over quite rapidly since 1980, and the younger new staff now include many Hispanics and Filipinos. Moreover, many of National's Anglo educators are culturally sensitive, with strong shared commitments to multiculturalism. The political culture of National today is also openly liberal and unified around the growth and well-being of all children, including newcomers to the community.

The Rosemead School District, unlike National, continues to be dominated by Anglo community leaders, board members, and senior school administrators. But its teachers and parents share across the several ethnic subcommunities a strong public positive value preference for multicultural education. And, like their counterparts in Isaac, teachers and senior administrators take pride in their familial style of relationships and communications. They are equally proud of their efforts to become culturally sensitive toward ethnic and language minorities. The political culture of Rosemead today is educationally progressive, inclusive, welcoming, and socially tolerant.

These features were noted in the course of our field visits. They are also evident from two of the rating scales. The Quality of Multiculturalism scale scores provide clues to a district's cultural configuration. Isaac and National schools were rated by our field observers as expressing a nearly total commitment to multicultural pluralism, intergroup social respect, and the conviction that the community is enhanced rather than diminished by the scope of its cultural and lingual diversity. Isaac scored 93% and National 89% on the QM scale, out of a possible 100%. Rosemead, at 70%, was above average.

Isaac, Rosemead, and National are communities whose public schools exemplify the importance of connecting parental involvement with student success in school (Lueder, 1989; Swap, 1990). Parents are treated by professional staff as equal partners in the educative process. Parents and other family members who have sufficient time and energy are enthusiastically recruited into school programs as volunteers and participants. Family members who cannot respond in this way because of poverty or poor health are often given support by school programs designed to assist the children in combination with supports for parents.

Community relations are also stressed in these school districts. School board members, administrators, and teachers respect the cultural integrity of the ethnically and lingually diverse households and do not presume to impose assimilationist pressures on children or adults.

## Stable and Low-Performing Districts

The National and Rosemead districts operate within the diverse California state context. Unlike that in Arizona, California's state education agency has been influential and active for most of the century. In 1983, soon after the consequences of Proposition 13 began to be felt and state hegemony over funding intensified, the California legislature passed its omnibus reform legislation of 1983. Many initiatives remain concentrated in the local districts (Little et al., 1987), but the role of the state of California expanded substantially between 1983 and 1990. Our study took place after the advent of the current economic depression in the state, however, and most state reform objectives had been deferred for want of resources. Within this volatile framework, then, National and Rosemead demonstrate the extent to which local culture can support initiatives toward improved education. In addition, the Isaac School District in Arizona has shown that local culture can support such initiatives.

None of the other eight school districts in the sample share all the cultural characteristics of high-performing districts: familial harmony, inclusiveness, and a strong public-service value. Some, like Washoe and Clark County districts, have strongly individualistic, competitive orientations. In contrast to Isaac, from which the Mormon settlers left, Washoe and Clark have been continuously dominated politically and religiously by the Mormon community, which includes many highly conservative members who disapprove strongly of bilingual instruction, multicultural education, and social mixing across ethnic groups.

Balsz, too, is Mormon-dominated historically. Its longstanding Hispanic community has always been subordinate to the Mormons politically and educationally, and today the city is sharply split between wealthy Anglo households and very poor minorities, who make up about one half of the population.

Fresno, despite its large percentage of minorities, huge population growth, and long history of hosting migrant and seasonal workers, remains for all intents and purposes a monocultural district whose leaders share a strong disposition toward assimilation into the Anglo mainstream. San Gabriel has always had a large Hispanic settlement but, somewhat like Fresno's, its political culture has been dominated by wealthy Anglo conservatives for decades.

Franklin McKinley does not maintain a distinctive local culture. Its agrarian roots have been severed. From 1960 to 1985, it was an enclave of housing and light industry (a food production plant) that supported factory and warehouse workers, but the plant is now closed. Vietnamese immigrants who came in the 1970s had little in common with the Hispanics who settled in the locality before them, and neither group had much in common culturally with the Cambodians who arrived in the 1980s. Franklin McKinley's school board has yet to adopt policies or hire senior administrators who know what to do about educating these essentially separate groups.

## COMMUNITIES AND RESOURCES

A school district's ability to make achievement gains is substantially affected by its history and culture. But distinctive community structural features may also differentiate between success and failure.

### Social Integration

Social integration refers to the interacting of different ethnic and income groups on a regular basis. It also refers to some degree of residential intermingling of subgroups.

The three highest performing districts are fairly well integrated socially but also maintain definite residential clustering of ethnic subcommunities. In all three, however, ethnically diverse families have lived across the street from one another or in houses next door to each other for many decades. Black and Hispanic subcommunities became established in Isaac 50 years ago, for example. National and Rosemead have included two or more ethnic groups in their communities with few apparent problems for generations. Rosemead has changed the most in population since 1970. Community power relations have been greatly affected by this; Rosemead has employed six superintendents during the past 8 years. Nevertheless, Rosemead organized itself on a communitywide basis to welcome its Asian and Latino newcomers late in the 1970s and did not reverse this friendliness later on. Scores on the Quality of Integration scale are also indicative. Isaac reached a score of 99%; National, 93%; and Rosemead, an above-average 78%.

Franklin McKinley, as an example of contrast among the stable districts, is both residentially and educationally separated into ethnic minority subgroups. It is surrounded by high-technology firms but does not serve households drawn from that labor force.

In low-performing districts, different distinctive subgroups do not interact much. In addition, ethnic minority groups tend to live in somewhat segregated clusters that are also defined by income level.

## District Size

A review of the literature on the relation between school-district size and achievement performance includes an empirical analysis of selected districts in California (Friedkin & Necochea, 1988). It identifies the alternative possibilities that shape a "size effect." For instance, increases in enrollment obviously correlate with increases in resources, and economies of scale materialize as well. Indeed, the evidence available from research literature published before 1988 leads one to infer that large districts can and ordinarily do deliver better quality educational services than small ones. Later studies, however, point to quite different conclusions.

On the negative side, very large districts often suffer from problems of coordination and control, and from vulnerability to the emergence of severe inequalities in the distribution of resources among schools and programs. The Friedkin and Necochea (1988) study found that among California districts, enrollment size and socioeconomic status of students interact powerfully, such that large districts with high-status students generate instructional and related service benefits, whereas those with low-status students do worse than smaller districts. In other words, the research suggests that the enrollment size of a district is somewhat of a "wash" in accounting for performance, except when student SES is introduced as a factor.

Walberg (1992), reviewing the district- and school-size issues, notes that from 1940 to 1990, the number of U.S. school districts decreased 87% (from 117,108 to 15,367), whereas average district enrollment increased over 10 times, from 217 students to 2,637. He finds a significant negative correlation between district size and two types of school achievement scores, and he reports that this finding, as well as the convergent correlation between school size and achievement, is supported by numerous other studies. Monk (1992) reviews the same evidence and finds it more complex and less obvious than does Walberg, but tending in essentially the same direction: Small is better, he concludes. Berlin et al. (1989) reach the same conclusion in a separate study. They summarize their findings this way: "People seem to learn, change, and grow in situations where they have some control, some personal influence, and some efficacy" (p. 10). Howley (1989) reaches a similar conclusion.

At the close of the 1980s, then, public school research and planning experts began to reverse a policy conviction they had upheld for 40 years—

that bigger districts, bigger schools, and bigger clusters of facilities and equipment resulted in increased and superior opportunities to learn as well as economies of scale.

The change represents a kind of intellectual culmination in the twin processes of urbanization and suburbanization. As thousands of rural villages became virtual ghost towns or were merged into cities and suburbs after World War II, metropolitan consolidation became the educational fashion. By 1980, the 100 largest urban districts in the nation enrolled one fourth of all public school students, and tens of thousands of village districts were consolidated into them and into the next 100 largest. The process itself became confounded by the need to increase school size to accommodate the baby boom (Dentler, 1987).

In any event, we have come now to the policy declaration—after much exploration and celebration of nonpublic schools and much conservative effort in California and Arizona alike to introduce school vouchers—that smaller is better, for districts as well as for schools and classrooms. It is apparent to us that district size depends for its effect on opportunities to learn on other cultural, economic, and school organizational factors; that it is not an important causal determinant in its own right. But any reader will note that our largest districts did not do as well as our smallest, in terms of change in achievement over time. This is distinctly the pattern for Fresno versus the three highest performing districts.

Fresno, Washoe, and Clark are perhaps too big and have grown far too much and too rapidly during the past decade to have been able to develop community infrastructures of facilities, programs, and services that are adequate for their residents. Washoe suffers currently from political strains between its ultraconservative power holders and its more moderate leaders. Clark maintains racially isolated schools for its residentially separated Black subcommunity, and Fresno's schools reflect its ethnically separate, isolated residential neighborhoods. Washoe and Clark show substantially less achievement decline than Fresno, however.

## District Expenditures

Both per pupil expenditures and teacher salaries are affected substantially by the political culture of each state. California has, until very recently, been significantly more munificent than Arizona in its public school investments, for example, and Nevada's two urban counties are higher investors than districts in either of the other two states. These counties are extraordinarily wealthy as a result of their world standing as gambling and entertainment centers; Las Vegas and Reno have tax money to burn, as one respondent said. This greater wealth is reflected in the data on resources shown in Table 4.1, especially in per pupil expenditures.

**Table 4.1 Budget Data for Sample Districts**

| District[a] | Per Pupil Expenditure[b] | Mean per Pupil Expenditure: 1990/1980[c] | Mean Teacher Salary | Salary % Mean |
|---|---|---|---|---|
| Isaac AZ | $2,433 | 1.41 | $31,007 | 99 |
| Rosemead CA | $3,424 | 1.63 | $30,767 | 98 |
| National CA | $3,776 | 1.64 | $33,373 | 107 |
| Franklin McK CA | NA | NA | NA | NA |
| Washoe Co. NV | $4,572 | 1.34 | $29,118 | 93 |
| Clark Co. NV | $4,260 | 1.30 | $31,446 | 100 |
| Balsz AZ | $2,750 | 1.37 | $28,016 | 89 |
| San Gabriel CA | $3,700 | NA | $35,549 | 113 |
| Fresno CA | $3,978 | 1.66 | $32,242 | 103 |
| Sunnyside AZ | $2,310 | 1.11 | $28,016 | 89 |
| Mt. View CA | $3,530 | 1.20 | $33,697 | 108 |

[a] Ranked from high positive achievement gains to high negative
[b] 1990 data, except for Washoe and Clark, in which 1989 data were used
[c] 1980 per pupil $ estimated from data from 1985 in some districts
NA = not available

Fresno, the second largest district in our sample and one of the five largest districts in California, spent far fewer dollars per pupil than did Washoe and Clark counties but a great deal more than was spent by the three high-gain districts.

Our sample is too small to permit generalizations, but it is obvious that Fresno spends more than 1.6 times per pupil than does Isaac. Our organizational analysis in Chapter 5 will show, however, that Isaac is not only far more prudent; it is also organized to optimize its utilization of extremely scarce resources. Millions of dollars of "in-kind" contributions are made in civic, leadership, and parental time and effort. Voluntarism is intense, and Isaac has many programs that operate as community-generated service activities.

We must keep in mind that although funding is important, what matters most about the communities is not size or financial resources but the extent to which the local culture and its extension into the public schools are supportive and inclusive of all resident children, youth, and adults.

Table 4.1 also supports the proposition that differences in dollar expenditures do not account for differences in district achievement score gains. The column showing per pupil expenditures for each district as a ratio of 1990 to 1980 supports the same proposition, but it also invites a second inference: All 11 districts increased their expenditures over the decade, in ratios ranging from 1.11 to 1.66, and the variation in magnitude of increases is not large. If we note that the increases are in ratio form and do not reflect dollars adjusted for cost inflation, it becomes obvious that Fresno, which underwent the largest enrollment increase among the districts, averaged a 16% increase each year during a period when inflation averaged 8% a year. The districts, when taken together, experienced extreme changes in enrollments and program impacts of enormous magnitude, yet received negligible increases in financial resources.

We also examined the federal dollar investments in the sample districts. There was no association between these and achievement gains. More important, 10 of the 11 districts where we obtained these data increased their federal resources substantially during the 1980s. Clark County had the lowest increase—125%—while Rosemead increased by 351%. Isaac increased at the midpoint for the 10—228%. The differences in levels of increased federal investment, most of them stemming from Chapter 1 and from bilingual supports, were also not associated with gains in achievement scores.

## CONCLUSIONS

Viewed in the light shed by their histories, local cultures, and community structures, the 11 districts are quite clearly bifurcated into either proactive, fluidly adaptive settings or change-resistant, reactive settings. Only one, Franklin McKinley, sits on a sort of cusp between the extremes that characterize these sources of school district policies and practices.

Two of the three high-performing districts have included small ethnic minority subcommunities for two generations or more that gradually increased to become a majority of the population. The third, Rosemead, was 96% Anglo until 1980. But as it began to change rapidly after 1980, it kept a cultural predisposition to be positive, welcoming, and adaptive rather than indifferent or resistant to change in receiving its student newcomers. Franklin McKinley, near San Jose, had also included a large Hispanic subcommunity for two generations. As Vietnamese and Cambodian families settled in Franklin McKinley in large numbers after 1980, however, the economy of the area was concomitantly dislocated and reduced. Franklin McKinley began to slide downward in economic resources and in community self-esteem as its community identity was merged with and then began to disappear into the sprawl of Silicon Valley. As part of this generally sharp distinction between adaptive/receptive and resistant/reactive districts, we also found that the former had leaders who consciously made their communities' activities and service systems welcoming and helpful to newcoming children, whereas the latter did not.

We have also concluded that very large districts face extra difficulties in hosting and helping newcomers, but that this issue, including the greater expenditures, is insignificant when compared with issues of community history and culture. A hospitable, educationally effective district inhabits a settlement in which diverse subcommunities are expected and welcomed and in which the norm of meeting the needs of all students is strong.

That factors other than local history and culture affect gains and losses in achievement is suggested by the fact that Mountain View scored high on the Quality of Integration and Quality of Multiculturalism scales yet suffered losses in mean achievement over the period. Something else— for instance, the organization of the district or its failure to develop appropriate educational and health services—may, as we shall show, account for the low performance of the Mountain View schools.

The more difficult question in developing a model for deliberate improvement in the education of ethnic and language minority students is whether school districts that have not yet changed, despite two decades of intense and urgent need for improvement, are doomed to fail in the future because of local history, local culture, or the community environment as a whole. Population size is part of community environment. Three of our largest districts—Fresno, Clark, and Washoe—have grown so large so fast and within a cultural context of resistance to multiculturalism that we expect improvements will be extremely difficult for them to attain in the near future.

We fear there may be a point of no return for public school districts that have grown very large very fast, that are receiving increasingly large numbers of disadvantaged children and youth from families in dire poverty, and that have been unresponsive historically to economic and societal changes. Current policy rhetoric and advocacy for administrative decentralization, charter schools, and privatization probably will not modify these patterns. Fresno is under strong political pressure at present to decentralize, for example, but we suspect that if it does so, its monocultural leaders will draw the subdistrict boundaries in ways that will reinforce the gap between the affluent Anglo and the impoverished Hispanic neighborhoods. In turn, structural dominance will be perpetuated. Size is not much of a problem in itself, although smallness is a help; but very large size, when compounded by failures to adapt to population changes and service needs over time, is probably educationally fatal.

As Jiobu (1990) has shown, adaptation for educational success also depends powerfully on which groups are coming to town. Rosemead

changed swiftly from a community predominantly Anglo to one predominantly minority, for example, but its success in improving its public
schools may be in part a function'of the fact that fewer than one fourth
of its households are below the federal poverty line. Another important
consideration is that a third of its recent arrivals have been middle- and
upper-income better-educated Southeast Asian and Chinese families.

Communities most severely impacted demographically by new, poorly
educated immigrants from rural Mexico and Latin America are those least
likely to have made rapid progress. However, Isaac is a major exception to
that generalization. Change in Isaac began early in the 1970s, and the
longer term Hispanic leadership was determined to find ways to be responsive. Districts with longstanding enclaves of racially isolated subpopula-
tions, like Clark County and San Gabriel, are less likely to find or even to
seek ways to improve their public schools.

We have reason to think that the forces of structural dominance in
public education generally work to translate (in a structural way) high SES
into high achievement, although in the Far West, the forces seem to
be slightly weakened in their impact on districts undergoing swift and
substantial demographic change. It may be that in our high-performing
districts, the otherwise profoundly negative effects of rising levels of household poverty and racial/ethnic and language minority status are counter-
vailed by distinctive forces of community history, culture, and school
organization. In our lowest performing districts, the expected effects of
structural dominance are compounded by negative features of the same
cultural and community forces.

Within contexts of rapid demographic and economic change, the leaders
of a public school district can also consciously and deliberately choose to
begin a new chapter in community history. A school board can find a way
to replace multi-ethnic divisions and political conflicts with a coalition
unified around child-centered programs. The ability of board members to
do this will depend somewhat, however, on the residential and economic
relations between the various status and ethnic subgroups in the community. Two of our low-performing districts are in severe economic decline.
We would not expect to see their leaders create adequate educational-
service bootstraps without funding. Fresno is a big city so filled with con-
tending factions and with breakdowns in its infrastructure due to exurban-
ization that positive changes in the way newcomers are received would
be nothing short of astonishing.

Even though they are subject to rather vast external events, economic
and political, the districts we sampled have not been coerced toward uni-
formity, for better or worse, by state policies. Their local distinctiveness

still shapes the course of their educational services more than do state policies, through the individual district characteristics discussed here.

How the best prospects for improvement in the delivery of services to disadvantaged children might be identified and reinforced is a question we revisit in Chapter 7. There we synthesize the influence of local history and culture with features of district and school organization and program data from the field study.

# 5
# District and School Organization

Many of the prevailing myths and ideologies about public education spring from a devolution of responsibility for student outcomes. That is to say, among the multitude of experts who speak for education, many of those who speak loudest assign final responsibility for what students do and do not know to what goes on in school, and ultimately to what teachers do in their classrooms. This view makes some sense, since the classroom is where one actually sees learning take place. On the other hand, by analogy, it is comparable to attributing the effectiveness of the U.S. Air Force to what mechanics do at Boeing Aircraft Company.

This chapter starts from the premise that the way classrooms and schools function is determined in many respects by the incentives and resources directed and controlled by a school district. The term *resources* is used here in its broadest sense to include information, power, and in-kind contributions from parents and other citizens and groups, as well as money and personnel.

The thrust of this chapter is that the school is a small and dependent component of a larger social system. However, consider the consequence of failing to focus on the larger system. From a seemingly endless stream of "effective schools" research, we have learned what good schools are like. We have also learned that there are some good schools and some bad ones. From that perspective, it follows that school improvement will have to take place one school at a time. The essential message is that schooling outcomes depend somewhat on the idiosyncrasies of particular schools and, for better or worse, on the idiosyncratic skills and interests of particular principals and teachers. The indisputable outcome of an idiosyncratic education system is that some individuals will benefit and others will lose.

Given the prevailing ideology that schools are responsible for learning outcomes, it is understandable that the voucher movement, charter schools, and other restructuring reform efforts have given up on top-down approaches. Instead, we are seeing school-by-school, teacher-by-teacher approaches to improve the education of 46 million children. Because no one knows what to do, we seem to be saying, let a few valiant and busy principals and teachers cope with the problems on their own.

This viewpoint may encourge and even recognize heroics, but it seems myopic. As Cuban (1984) has observed, the current preoccupation with the local school site and the principal's leadership obscures the pivotal role of school boards and superintendents in finding and allocating resources and legitimating reform efforts.

For purposes of this chapter, the 11 site reports were reviewed in search of district policies and organizational structures and patterns that seemed to have had some impact on student test scores. Site reports were read in three groups, formed on the basis of how much test scores had improved, as described in Chapter 2. Positive and negative attributes that were described in each case were recorded. This step yielded a list of attributes that seemed reasonable candidates to consider in this effort to explain the variation in outcomes (see Figure 5.1 at end of this chapter).

We then reread the cases, using the attribute list in Figure 5.1 as a mental overlay, seeking to detect those that were present or absent in more than one situation. The first section of the chapter reports interpretations based on these procedures and presents an ideal type model. Although specific attributes that stood out as important are mentioned, the really critical result is the profile, that is, the way particular attributes are combined.

The approach taken here assumes that some otherwise positive attributes will remain dormant unless set in motion by certain others, and that the presence of a few detrimental conditions can overwhelm otherwise favorable circumstances. Furthermore, some attributes can compensate for the absence of others. Finally, the importance of particular attributes and clusters probably will vary from place to place depending on local circumstances.

## AN IDEAL TYPE MODEL

The characteristics that make up our profile are present, hypothetically, in the most extreme successful case, an ideal model that we can use as a standard against which to compare our 11 sites. However, because success is a relative concept, a district can be moderately successful when some favorable characteristics are not present or, alternatively, when some negative attributes are present. The model or, less pretentiously, "scenario" followed in the successful districts operates more or less as follows.

## Community Characteristics

A school district is shaped by, and thus reflects, the community it represents. The community forms parameters that virtually dictate the problems a school system faces and what it can and cannot do. Two dimensions of community are especially critical: the degree of impact it faces and its core structure. Impact refers to the numbers of newcomers and the heterogeneity resulting from growth and turnover in the student body, poverty, and economic losses. Core structure consists of size and correlates of size, support for education, and cohesiveness (i.e., absence of extreme segmentation among strata and groups).

**Degree of Impact.** Impact is a product of the number and distinctiveness of cultural groups entering a community within a relatively short time span. In the most manageable scenario, groups with one or, at most, a few non-English languages have settled in large numbers. However, the level of poverty and the educational backgrounds of the newcomers are also of obvious importance. In the Far West, communities now hosting new immigrants from impoverished areas of rural Mexico and war-torn countries of Central America face overwhelming challenges.

In one relatively unsuccessful district, 20 different language groups are present in the schools; many students are very recent arrivals who speak no English. Perhaps no district is prepared to handle such an overwhelming burden. By comparison, in another—successful—district, there is only one large language group, and that group has been present since the mid-1970s. In the ideal case, then, the impact is limited to the gradual growth of a known group rather than the introduction of many new language groups. There seems to be a historical threshold, however, in that minorities who settled in communities decades ago were usually employed in subservient occupations and sequestered within specific areas of their community. Such long periods of Anglo dominance, as we noted before, seem to desensitize communities to the needs of new minorities.

**Core Structure.** The ideal district tends to be relatively small and homogeneous. It has passed tax and bond issues recently, has few serious tensions among racial/ethnic groups, and has parent committees not dominated by Anglos.

The district-size factor requires additional comment, because the issue is more complicated than portrayed in our simplified ideal type. As discussed in Chapter 4, although small districts in the study sample are generally more effective than larger ones, that outcome cannot be attributed to their size alone. Some scholars do treat size as a causal variable, but most authorities regard it as a concomitant associated with (and often masking) a host of other causal variables (Monk, 1992). Therefore, although small districts may be doing relatively well, size per se is not necessarily the main reason.

For example, as pointed out in Chapter 4, very large districts are often segmented and suffer from problems of coordination and control, but the same problems often prevail in smaller districts as well. Simply reducing their size will not solve all the problems. Instead, big districts can take certain measures to offset their difficulties. For example, there are severe inequities in the distribution of resources among schools and programs in big districts. Resources can be distributed more equitably without downsizing.

To take another example, the bureaucratic hierarchies of specialists common in big districts frequently diffuse and obscure responsibility for outcomes. Division of labor in these districts is certainly a challenge and the potential for oversight is immense, but lack of accountability is not an inevitable outcome. In principle, big districts can overcome such problems by implementing other corrective measures. Therefore, care should be taken not to interpret the disadvantages associated with bigness as a mandate for breaking up large districts into smaller ones.

Our field research suggests, as the profiles of district organization presented later in the chapter explain, that both school restructuring and district decentralization, accompanied by site-based management, seldom get at the root of the challenges faced by high-impact urban schools. The research and hortatory reform literature on these approaches grew substantially between 1989 and 1993 (Brown, 1992; Rowley, 1992; Stinnette, 1993), but our evidence, like most of that from the sources cited, suggests that more holistic approaches are needed and that moving authority downward without reconstituting the central administrative leadership (Hirsh & Sparks, 1991) will result in very few improvements.

## School Board Attributes

The composition, goals, and behavior of the school board are important for successful districts. Boards are pivotal in the change process; they buffer changes in the community, either by ignoring them or by forcefully addressing them. The role they choose depends on their composition. The rate and pattern of change in a school board frequently differ markedly from those in the community.

School board attributes can be divided into three dimensions: composition, goals, and supportive behavior of the members. These attributes, as they play out in the successful districts, can be summarized as follows:

1. Groups that have recently arrived in a district are represented on the board. In addition, Anglos on the board do not represent a special constituency opposed to change.
2. Board members recognize the need to accommodate recent arrivals and have given the superintendent a mandate to change the district to do so. There is consensus on this goal and, therefore, no permanent rifts among the members. They do not see new minorities as threats, nor do they worry about losing control of the district.
3. Board members vocally support the superintendent. They may disagree but do not fight frequently among themselves.

In a changing community, turnover in board membership is an important key to the speed and effectiveness with which a district accommodates new arrivals. Although some longtime board members adapt to new circumstances, as a general rule longtime residents do not make the best representatives of new groups. Board turnover also can reflect more basic changes in a community that is ready for change.

Note again the importance of patterns in the above profile. A board's vocal support for a superintendent who is not committed to change is a negative attribute. Support for change, not blind allegiance to a superintendent, is what is important. Similarly, absence of rifts among board members will lead to improved schools only if the board is committed to accommodate new populations of students. On the other hand, a board can be paralyzed by one or two members who are determined to oppose changes supported by the majority.

Board members should visit schools regularly, become acquainted with the principals, and know the names of some teachers. Board members who visit with teachers and students often gain insights and information. But perhaps more important, such visits can crystallize a board member's abstract commitment to education. Ultimately, visiting schools is perhaps simply something that deeply concerned board members want to do.

## Attributes of the Superintendent

It has been observed that in a growing number of American school districts, school superintendents are increasingly initiating fundamental school reform (Hallinger & Edwards, 1992). Accordingly, appointing the superintendent is probably the single most important decision a school board makes. However, the superintendent should be looked upon as an instrument, an extension of the board's will, not as some kind of heroic, charismatic leader. The effective-schools literature gives high priority to that vague and illusive quality called "leadership." However, the superintendent's actions are inseparable from the school board's mandate. On the one hand, a board that wants something to happen looks for someone who is equally committed and prepared to make it happen. On the other, that person relies on the board to support programs and decisions.

The attributes of superintendents in successful districts fall into three categories. These are personal attributes and behavior, personal priorities, and interpersonal relationships.

At least three personal attributes are characteristic of superintendents who manage successful districts. These people are visionary and willing to take some risks, they are widely regarded as competent and informed, and they work long hours.

However, a superintendent's personal priorities are probably more important than her or his personal traits. Priorities can be divided into two components. The first is a commitment to meet the challenge of cultural diversity. This commitment is reflected a number of ways. Of special importance, a superintendent acknowledges the existence of cultural and language challenges in the district and advocates addressing them aggressively. In contrast to this ideal, some superintendents are inclined to ignore or deny such problems, or they gloss them over in order to preserve their public relations image. Moreover, cultural diversity within the community is viewed by an effective superintendent as a strength, and as an enriching experience, rather than as a threatening invasion. Finally, a successful superintendent is guided by the principles of achieving equity and helping disadvantaged, at-risk students.

The second component of a superintendent's personal priorities is pragmatic. He or she must be firm-minded and determined to actually implement instructional programs. This requirement goes well beyond merely endorsing and legitimating cultural norms, which some authors choose to emphasize (e.g., Coleman & LaRocque, 1988). It involves mobilizing the power and authority associated with the office. He or she works aggressively to find the means to achieve the desired programs. Without this component, priorities amount to little more than good intentions or ceremonial lip service.

For example, a superintendent who is committed to bilingual education gives high priority to hiring bilingual teachers and finding resources to pay extra for that skill. He or she not only stresses the importance of students' learning English but also provides programs to help them do so. More generally, the superintendent seeks out funds and finds creative ways to reallocate available resources within the budget to meet instructional priorities (as opposed to lamenting the lack of money for instructional programs).

The third dimension of an effective superintendent is intense involvement in a wide web of relationships within the district and community at large as well as within state and federal agencies. This dimension has these components: accessibility, collaboration, participation, and cosmopolitan ties.

The first quality, accessibility, means that he or she is not sheltered behind assistants, secretaries, and appointment calendars. The superintendent's door should usually be open to parents and others, or at least open at publicized times.

The superintendent collaborates with individual school board members outside of formal meetings and with other members of the administrative staff. The superintendent also works closely with a variety of community leaders on projects relating to the school.

A superintendent who meets the participation ideal takes an active role in critical administrative decisions, of which selecting key personnel is perhaps the most important. Superintendents of successful districts handpick their principals and even interview most new teachers. In addition, they may interview other teachers at important career stages, such as tenure. These activities are very different from the all-too-common practice of delegating responsibilities and forgetting about them until problems arise.

Finally, an effective superintendent maintains close relationships with all major segments of the community, including newly arrived groups, as opposed to confining his or her connections to the dominant sector. Moreover, he or she is able to find sources of support and funding within the community (e.g., businesses, social agencies, colleges), the state, or at the federal level. Accordingly, the superintendent travels. The critical importance of district size is apparent in some of these attributes. It is nearly impossible for a superintendent of a large district to interview teachers. However, the chief administrator must not lose track of critically important delegated functions. In a large district, the superintendent can review qualifications of newly appointed teachers, interview some of them at random, talk regularly with the personnel director, and take an active role in appointing principals. Also, in a large district, accessibility must be achieved through formal arrangements, such as biannual neighborhood meetings or open sessions before or after school board meetings.

The importance of commitment to the goals of improving education for minorities and finding the necessary means to do so cannot be overemphasized. In some districts, the attention of well-meaning administrators has been diverted by controversial, expensive, or time-consuming building programs or efforts to install instructional technologies.

The ethnicity of the superintendent is conspicuously absent in this discussion. It is true that Isaac, a predominantly Hispanic community, had a

Hispanic superintendent. His background undoubtedly prepared him to work sensitively with that community. However, the previous superintendent, an Anglo woman, was equally committed to the same objectives. Moreover, in one community a superintendent of Hispanic background was so closely tied to the traditional Hispanic power structure that he ignored newly arrived Hispanic groups. Therefore, although a minority background can help in some instances, it does not appear to be a necessary attribute for a superintendent of a successful district.

## Attributes of Other Administrators

Although the superintendent is the key player, other members of the administrative staff provide necessary support and backup. Moreover, in areas where the superintendent has some deficiencies, the staff can often compensate. Their desirable characteristics have the same dimensions as those already described for the superintendent, namely, personal attributes and behavior, personal priorities, and interpersonal relationships. Rather than repeating the observations already made, we confine this discussion to some supplementary remarks.

The superintendent's behavior provides a model that at least some other administrators may emulate. In particular, in successful districts, some staff members work protracted hours alongside the superintendent. Also, they generally respect and support the superintendent, are not openly critical, and do not attempt to undercut the district's objectives and programs.

Because superintendents of successful districts take an active role in selecting personnel, it would be surprising if at least some of these people did not share the priorities of the board and superintendent. However, even in districts where the superintendent is not actively committed to providing good bilingual programs, a staff member who acts as a strong advocate for minorities can make an important difference. A mark of a successful district is that most administrators say they work as a team, meaning that they communicate frequently, are aware of each other's activities, and share information and assignments.

## Authority and the Incentive System

Because of the prevailing influence of the priorities and commitments of the school board and superintendent in successful districts, it is impossible to describe the authority structure apart from the incentives (rewards, pressures, and punishments) provided for principals, teachers, and others in key positions. This topic can be described in terms of these components: staffing pattern, what is expected of principals, balance of autonomy, and control.

The successful districts of Isaac, National, and Rosemead have lean administrative staffs. This pattern reflects, in part, the small size of such districts. However, it is also a consequence of the priorities already mentioned. Isaac, for example, was able to pay its teachers well, in part because the administrative staff was not allowed to grow as fast as those in many other comparable districts in the state.

In the most successful of the 11 districts, principals are given recognition for the considerable time they spend working with members of the community and programs provided for parents. They display an unwavering commitment to bilingual education and give top priority to hiring bilingual teachers. And they are all intensely involved in the daily affairs of their school, spending most of their time in the hallways, playgrounds, and classrooms. They are familiar with what various teachers are doing in their classes at any particular time.

In the ideal case, autonomy is always conditional, available only to the extent its use is consistent with district priorities. Principals and teachers have autonomy and latitude to run their schools and classrooms as they think best. However, they are not left entirely on their own. Rather, the district provides incentives, in the form of praise, recognition, and even bonuses. They may be rewarded for working with the community, taking creative approaches to instruction, meeting the needs of language and cultural minorities, maintaining good attendance records (in the case of teachers), and the like. It is clearly understood that a principal or a teacher does not have the option of neglecting the district's priorities. However, everyone is encouraged to take initiative in finding better ways to meet them.

It is important to understand the behavior of principals and teachers as an extension of district priorities and personnel policies rather than as the fortuitous gathering of some good people in one district. The superintendent handpicks principals and teachers who are committed to the right goals, then provides incentives to be sure employees fulfill them. There is control and close monitoring of progress toward priorities. Freedom is restricted by norms and clear expectations. Autonomy is available only to the extent it is likely to contribute to the goal of serving cultural and language minorities. What we are describing is fundamentally different from the premise of much site-based management, which permits principals and teachers to decide for themselves what should be done.

## DISTRICT PROFILES

Patterns among the key attributes can be readily discerned within the individual school districts, as the highlights described here will demonstrate. Although we originally identified three high performers, for the comparative purposes of this discussion we concentrate on the four districts with the largest increase in test scores (high achievers) and the four with the largest decline (low achievers). As described in Chapter 2, we classified Franklin McKinley as a stable district because it showed only slight improvement in test scores. However, because it ranked fourth overall in the performance list, we decided to look at this case more closely as a possibly marginal high performer.

## High-Performing Districts

Four districts are described below. All have a disproportionately high number of positive attributes that characterize the ideal type model.

**Isaac.** This district has been consistently supported by voters who passed two bonds to build three schools without state aid. No clearly discernible group in the community consistently exercises disproportionate power and there are no visible cleavages among power blocs. Ethnic tensions are notably absent. The board runs the district without significant interference from other power holders in the community.

The five-person board includes an Anglo who has served for 30 years. However, the board acquired two elected Hispanic members for the first time in the early 1980s. When it added a third Hispanic member, the process of rapid and deep change began. The administrative team and the majority of the board are now Hispanics who share intense conviction about the importance of maintaining a multicultural school system with particular emphasis on Spanish bilingual programs. Board members visit schools regularly and know many of the teachers personally.

When the Isaac board appointed an Anglo woman as superintendent, it also gave her a strong mandate to implement her vision of curriculum reform, parental involvement, teacher empowerment, and multiculturalism. She, in turn, appointed a Hispanic, who grew up nearby, as a principal and then as personnel director and assistant superintendent. He succeeded her as superintendent, a position he holds today. When he was appointed, he immediately inaugurated sweeping changes in personnel, programs, and planning. This superintendent is active in Hispanic organizations throughout the state and has used his influence to pressure the state for an alternative achievement test. Within Isaac, he uses a parent advisory council representing all of the schools, and he visits schools frequently, making himself accessible to teachers and students. Under his administration, each principal works with small clusters of parents.

A centerpiece of the superintendent's reform strategy has been to recruit competent, dedicated, bilingual teachers committed to the district's reform priorities, including experience-based classroom teaching and community outreach activities. He interviews all prospective teaching candidates and actively recruits from schools and college campuses. One third of the teachers he has hired are members of minority groups, and he has appointed several minority principals.

Problems with gangs, drugs, and crime are readily acknowledged by the administration and board. As a show of force, a police detective is housed conspicuously in the junior high school. Several parents expressed their belief that the district has been relatively successful in curbing the gang problem within the past 2 years.

The headquarters organization is simple and lean, consisting of 12 administrators and 15 additional support personnel. Every school has access to a counselor, a nurse, special services, and bilingual programs. This district aggressively seeks and obtains funding from almost every conceivable source, but especially from federal programs. It generates more than 14% of its budget from contracts and grants. Consequently, a seemingly endless variety of programs are either in operation or in planning stages. Businesses sponsor some programs. The district publishes a monthly newsletter for parents in both Spanish and English.

Isaac is unified around very explicit educational and social goals. Administrators, principals, and teachers are delegated specific and substantial areas of authority and autonomy to carry out their responsibilities within the constraints of these goals.

Teacher salaries are a high priority; Isaac is one of the three highest paying districts among the 55 within Maricopa County and the Phoenix area. Teachers have high morale, notwithstanding the fact that many of them work long hours. Veteran and new teachers alike trust administrators and cooperate with them. They are respected as professionals and given some autonomy over their classes and opportunities to participate in curriculum decisions. They, in turn, treat students with respect and affection. Certified bilingual teachers receive a $1,000 bonus. Each school has a large number of Spanish bilingual teachers, administrators, and other staff, including parent volunteers. School staffs also include Anglo and African American teachers and administrators, and a larger than customary complement of males. Teachers have access to a variety of in-service programs.

In no Isaac school is any ethnic group or social class sequestered, tracked, grouped, or treated differently by program. Isaac uses some add-on programs, but LEP instruction is fully integrated into the school routines in addition. Even a self-contained Hispanic bilingual program at one school assures high crossover between this program and English-only classes.

The community has supported new programs over the past 15 years, and, in turn, the district has anticipated and readily acknowledged problems as they have developed. The district is not paralyzed by wrenching dissension. A key to the district's success is the uneventful transition within the school board from predominately Anglo to predominately Hispanic representation. As mentioned before, the board is now headed by a local Hispanic from within the district. However, the forceful influence of the former superintendent, an Anglo woman, is evidence that the interests of ethnic groups can be represented by Anglos. What is important is that the minority group is fairly represented, which can be best assured if it retains the ultimate power.

Isaac relies heavily on outside funding to support its programs, as we noted. The superintendent and others in the district are extremely sophisticated about finding and obtaining money. However, they are also serious about implementing and maintaining the programs and providing inservice for teachers. Programs that involve parents have a high priority.

In summary, we see that this small, relatively harmonious community provides an ideal setting to meet the challenges it faces. The changeover in ethnic composition has been going on for 15 years, giving the district time to prepare to cope with a single-language group. The superintendent, who is the hub of a circle of relationships with groups in the community and throughout the state, has clearly been the major force behind Isaac's preparations for the language minorities that have swept into the district in recent years. The current superintendent has taken advantage of the momentum for change he inherited from his predecessor and, more important, a very supportive and cohesive board. Indeed, he was a major figure during that regime as well. Many new teachers have been hired, and he has virtually controlled all hiring for the past decade as he advanced from personnel director to assistant superintendent to superintendent. His key strategy has been to personally hire all teachers and to appoint as many principals as possible.

The district has made teacher salaries a high priority, deliberately keeping the central administration lean to help pay for them. Its commitment to bilingual education and community outreach programs has been clear and unwavering. In addition, the superintendent keeps in close touch with the schools, so he can monitor progress toward those goals. This district has not simply turned over the problems and priorities to local schools. Rather, the schools exercise their autonomy within the district priorities and guidelines.

**National.** A small, transient community near San Diego (with a population of about 6,200 students), National serves as a base for immigrants and military families. No racial tension is visible, but there is some gang activity. The unemployment rate is high, and many of the families are on welfare. About a third of the students in the district are limited-English-proficient, which represents a 50% increase over the past decade.

Anglos dominated the school board until the mid-1980s. However, it now consists of two Hispanics, two Anglos, and one Filipino. Most of them have served for several years and are respected in the community. They are supportive of the superintendent. The superintendent, a Hispanic, grew up in the area. He is highly respected in the community, as was his predecessor. The board considers him well qualified, visionary, and innovative—a man with a clear sense of what he wants and firm-minded about implementing his program. He emphasizes the importance of a set of core values that are being promoted throughout the district. They include meaningful parent involvement through home-school partnerships, shared leadership and communication, staff development, and a student-centered curriculum designed for critical thinking. Recently, he handpicked several new principals who share his vision. They describe him as very accessible.

The superintendent, along with other staff, also works closely with members of the National City community. He is involved in civic activities and has established partnership with members of the city council, Chamber of Commerce, and some business people. Parents serve on important advisory committees, and they conduct and participate in workshops that teach them how to help their children. Each school publishes a bilingual newsletter for parents.

Besides the superintendent, there is only one other Hispanic in the central office. However, the central office staff is very stable and generally regarded as highly committed. Staff members, who have worked in the district from 10 to 30 years, share a vision of what they want the district to be, and they work as a team, in close cooperation with the superintendent.

National has been successful in securing outside funding; consequently, there are many funded programs operating, including a restructuring planning grant. In addition, National has a needs assessment center designed to screen, diagnose, and place children new to the district. A wide range of assessments are used.

Bilingual programs have been in place for 20 years (see Chapter 3). A concerted effort has been made to hire and support bilingual teachers, and about 30% are certified bilingual. Thirty-five percent of the teaching staff have minority backgrounds. More than one fourth of the teachers are Hispanic. Most (80%) have master's degrees, and a sizable number (14%) have doctorates. They work long hours but appear to have good morale and come across as caring, devoted, and cooperative. The district provides valuable in-service programs and resources, and it has a mentor-teacher program to provide each teacher with support and feedback.

**Rosemead.** The Rosemead School District goes back over 100 years. The city is small, with a population of 52,000, including 3,200 students.

Rosemead continues to be dominated by Anglo community leaders, board members, and senior school administrators. The school board and superintendent work well together, although tension was created between the board and the previous superintendent, who wanted to control the board. The board president's priority is for the board to be accessible to the public. It has an "open door" policy and holds 30-minute public hearings before each board meeting.

The Anglo superintendent is regarded by principals and teachers as open-minded and willing to listen. He visits every school in the district four times each year, and he works closely with members of the community through several committees concerned with bilingual education, community growth, strategic planning, and budget. He also works with members of the city council and solicits local businesses to sponsor school activities. He has secured grants and programs for students who speak limited English. The district has been very aggressive about obtaining funds from all levels of government. The superintendent personally interviews all prospective teachers, striving to recruit credentialed ESL teachers and other teachers capable of teaching LEP and NEP students. Teachers who pass an English Language Development test are given a $500 bonus.

The central administration consists of only four people, one of whom is minority (a Japanese female). There are no Hispanics in the administration, with the exception of one vice principal. However, all four of the administrators in the central office regard the ethnic diversity of the community as a positive attribute. Committees in the district are actively planning for still more projected growth in language minorities. Also, newsletters and other forms of communication are produced and translated into other languages.

Rosemead's teaching staff is predominately Anglo (86%); only 9% are Hispanic. Nearly half the teachers in the district have been hired within the past 5 years. Only 8 of the district's 123 teachers have bilingual certificates in Spanish, but these 8 are spread out among the schools. Meanwhile, ongoing staff-development programs are helping all teachers prepare for the changing student population. The goal is for every teacher to learn to work with language minorities without watering down the content of courses for ESL students.

Teachers at Rosemead share with parents representing several ethnic subcommunities a strong commitment to multicultural education. The teachers have good morale, are supported by their principals, and hold high expectations for their students. However, teachers are not close to the community. Some teachers complain that parents, especially Asians, are becoming less involved with the schools and that many lack parenting skills. However, parents continue to be active in the tutoring program for immigrant students.

Rosemead resembles the ideal type in many respects. It is small, has a long history, and has only two languages represented in addition to English. Board members are not split among themselves and do not cater to different constituencies. A previous struggle between the board and the former superintendent has been overcome; they now work in harmony. The board and administration are responsive to the community and regard cultural diversity as a strength rather than a threat.

The superintendent works with the community through committees, secures the assistance of influential members of the community for his programs, and aggressively goes after outside money. His priorities are clear and firmly fixed on helping disadvantaged language minorities. Perhaps most important, he keeps his finger on the key decisions, including pushing for bilingual programs and hiring new staff.

**Franklin McKinley.** This is a medium-size district (10,000 students) located within a large city (population about 700,000). There are some overt racial tensions in the district. The community is divided into distinct areas inhabited predominantly by Hispanics, Southeast Asians, African Americans, or Anglos. In addition, however, are small integrated pockets of middle-income residents from all nationalities and races.

The district is divided into factions regarding two controversies: one over plans to add grades 7 and 8 to two elementary schools, the other over an expensive new district service center. The former issue has triggered some expressions of racism and social elitism, because the plan would require Anglo students to mix with minorities at the middle school. Critics of the center, which provides comprehensive services (including childcare, probation, and truancy services; counseling; and health facilities), question its cost, its adequacy, and whether authorization was granted to build it in the first place.

The Franklin McKinley school board consists of two Anglos, two Asians, and one African American. Although the district is predominantly Hispanic, no Hispanics are on the board. It is dominated by the superintendent, who usually gets her own way in contests with board members. She has been able to push through controversial projects that the board initially disapproved.

The superintendent, a capable Anglo woman, was in the position for a decade before leaving under pressure (this occurred after our site visit). She visited each school annually and met with representatives from each school bimonthly. As the key decision maker in the district, she was the center of controversy, either liked or disliked by different constituencies. The main criticism was that she placed too much emphasis on technology while allowing services for the disadvantaged language minorities to languish for "lack of funding." She did not seem to be aware of the extensive demographic changes that had occurred in Franklin. A new school board majority has expressed dissatisfaction with the lack of programs addressing the needs of language minority students.

Of the 12 central office staff, 9 are Anglos. There is only one Hispanic with management responsibilities in the central office. The coordinator of language development acts as an advocate for LEP students. However, his recommendations are generally overlooked or compromised by other priorities within the district. Similarly, the principals are dominated and overruled by the superintendent. Consequently, their decisions often do not reflect their own judgment but rather their deference to higher authorities.

The district is fiscally solvent, and the administration has the support of the school board. There are several business partnerships and other programs. The new service center provides help for the economically disadvantaged. However, because technology is the major priority, not much money is left for language programs, which are a low priority. The language programs in operation resemble approaches in use 15 years ago, based on ESL individual pull-out programs that provide as little as 15 to 30 minutes of daily assistance (see also Chapter 3). There is no provision for teaching native-language literacy. One administrator endorsed the old-line English-only movement based on an immersion approach for LEP students. Teachers in mainstream classrooms with minimal language training must struggle on their own.

Twenty-nine percent of the teachers are members of minority groups. Few teachers are bilingual, even among those certified for the ESL program. Some teachers express a great deal of hostility toward their central administration and their principal because there are too many students who need help with language and other special problems. They feel they are expected to do too much in overcrowded classrooms, with too little support from the district. They particularly resent having taken cuts in salary to help finance the service center. Many of the veteran teachers retain traditional ideas and resist making changes.

The reasons for Franklin McKinley's marginal status on achievement gains become clearer: It has few attributes that match the ideal type. Although minorities are represented on this school board, the dominant language minority is not. However, what may be decisive is the powerful hold the superintendent has over this board. Again, the influences of the superintendent and school are clearly visible. Just as a forceful superintendent can make a district responsive to new types of students, so too can a superintendent back priorities that deflect attention from helping newcomers.

We can see in Franklin McKinley that harmony within the board, close, supportive relationships with the superintendent, and forceful leadership from the superintendent do not necessarily, by themselves, lead to a responsive school district prepared to cope with new challenges. Those traits must feed into a viable set of priorities.

However, the critical fact is that in this district with students from many ethnic, racial, and cultural backgrounds, there is little evidence of a serious, dedicated effort to serve all types of students. The district has done very little to welcome new language minorities. That has not been a priority of the superintendent or the school board, and therefore the task of meeting the needs of LEP students has been relegated to school-site administrators and teachers, most of whom likewise have no interest and none of the necessary technical knowledge. Each school was left free to address the issues in its own idiosyncratic manner.

This could explain both why this district did not show much improvement and why it did not do as badly as one might have expected from the district-level profile. That is, in instances where the principal and school-site council felt strongly about assisting disadvantaged students, they found ways to allocate the necessary funds. But when school administrators did not give such assistance high priority, the disadvantaged suffered. Similarly, whereas some teachers went out of their way to adapt their instruction to the characteristics of children in their classes, many others presented lessons as if all students were fluent in English.

The net result of this casual decentralized approach is that the achievements of some schools get washed out by the failures of others. And, of course, the reverse: Franklin did not totally fail thanks to the valorous efforts of a few schools. Hence, taken as a whole, the district totters on the fine line between positive improvement and little change. This is a telling indictment of decentralized approaches to reform, currently so highly—and misguidedly—touted.

## Low-Performing Districts

The four districts described in this section have disproportionately more negative attributes than the improving districts. They show little match with the ideal type model.

**Sunnyside.** This district, near Tucson, exemplifies many of the attributes that virtually guarantee failure. As noted in Chapter 4, Sunnyside's community history differs fundamentally from that of high-achieving districts. As a fringe barrio for Tucson's Hispanic households, the district currently has a predominately Hispanic enrollment (72%). Medium-sized Sunnyside (enrollment 13,500) is split into two distinct communities, one traditionally Hispanic that controls the district, the other made up of new arrivals from Mexico. Some parents regarded the new arrivals as invaders, fearing the Mexicans would take control of the schools. There is a lively back-to-basics movement that some residents believe will segregate and further divide the school system. The existing back-to-basics elementary school is disproportionately Anglo and offers no special-education or bilingual programs.

The board president, a Hispanic, is closely linked to the traditional community. Newcomers' interests are not represented on the board, which is highly politicized and dominated by "local politicians." Board members are so accessible and responsive to the special interests or complaints of individuals from the established, traditional community that they are ineffective in dealing with the community as a whole.

The superintendent, regarded by some as "one of the good ol' boys," represents only the traditional Hispanic community. He does his job, but throughout 20 years in the district, he has not demonstrated an educational vision. He is preoccupied with putting up a good public front, which includes minimizing problems with gangs, family transience, and poverty. His solution to learning problems is to lower grade requirements for extracurricular activities.

As the district has grown, so has the bureaucracy. The central administration is widely criticized for being detached and noncommunicative and for failing to work on problems facing students. The bilingual director, a potential force for change, is considered by some as too weak for her job. The superintendent, the director of bilingual education, and one other central office administrator visit schools on a regular basis. However, the other administrators do not, and board members are rarely seen in schools. The administration blames low student outcomes on the students' social backgrounds, home situations, parents' values, and other external factors. A monthly newsletter is written predominantly in English. Many teachers are from minority backgrounds (28%), but they come from the traditional community.

The district has launched several major programs in the past decade, but they are widely ridiculed as superficial "jokes," introduced primarily to satisfy state guidelines and without the benefit of follow-up. Until recently, the existing programs relied on pull-out strategies and did not serve some minorities in the district (see Chapter 3). The teachers, whom the board president accuses of failing to understand their responsibility to students, are overwhelmed by this parade of new and fashionable programs. They lament the lack of guidance or support from the district, complain that the district has not provided the appropriate textbooks and other materials, and express desperation as they try to teach the new student population.

Despite problems within Sunnyside, one of its schools has been recognized for its exemplary programs. Again, however, parents are resentful because the board has been slow to acknowledge the school's achievements.

This district is a prime example of what can happen when the task of meeting new challenges is left up to schools and teachers without direction and backing from the school district. Even though at least one school seemed to be doing a good job, it was not given much recognition, and other schools were adrift. The case of Sunnyside also suggests one reason districts avoid facing up to the challenges of educating new student populations, namely, paralysis resulting from political divisions with the community. The root problem is the cleavage within the dominant minority community itself, and the superintendent's allegiance to the traditional power structure to the neglect of newcomers' interests.

**Fresno.** This is an ethnically diverse, stratified, large Central Valley community, consisting mostly of ethnic/racial minorities. Fresno has always had a large Hispanic population. In the 1980s, substantial Asian and Southeast Asian groups arrived. The district has experienced a dramatic growth of 30,000 students over the past decade.

Notwithstanding these vital changes in the student population, the curriculum and programs in the district have not changed in the last 10 years. As the teaching force grew by 61%, the percentage of teachers from minority backgrounds increased by only 15%, despite the high rate of ethnic minorities in the community. Few district administrators saw recruiting more minorities as a high priority.

These rigidities can be attributed to Fresno's power structure. The city is split into distinct sections consisting of, respectively, predominately middle-class Anglos, middle-class Hispanics, poor Hispanics (who make up 36% of the city), Asians, African Americans, and other nationalities. Middle-class Anglo parents with an assimilation mentality have managed to maintain control of the bodies that govern the district and the schools their children attend. They resist the idea of "catering" to students from different cultures who speak languages other than English.

Although two of the seven members have Hispanic backgrounds, the Fresno board of education is dominated by Anglos. The president of the school board, who along with other board members is preoccupied with financial issues, admits at times to not knowing exactly how to cope with problems in the district. The board inherited a budget that previous administrations had seriously mismanaged. It is attempting to develop a more collaborative relationship with the administration, which in the past had controlled the board. Other administrators are decidedly critical of the way this board has handled some of its responsibilities.

Fresno's superintendent, an Anglo male with experience throughout California, is new to the area, as is his deputy, an Anglo woman. There are four Hispanics and two African Americans in the central administration. Some administrators express concern about students who are having difficulty with English, but not to the extent that they act as advocates for them. Their goal is for students to become fluent in English, but bilingual programs have not been set up to help them make the transition from their native language. At most, there are some ESL pull-out programs that provide up to a half-hour of assistance per day. However, a monthly newsletter to parents and the community is translated into several languages.

Teachers in Fresno have, on average, many years of experience. They have influence within their respective schools, but they do not participate in setting district policy. Although in-service is available, teachers must request it. Very few in-service sessions on LEP strategies were given.

Only 19% of the teaching staff belong to a minority, and the few bilingual teachers and part-time bilingual aides are spread so thinly across various classrooms that students do not receive much native-language support. There are only a few bilingual classes, and few office personnel in the district speak Spanish. Despite the cultural diversity within schools, teachers make no special provisions in their classes, instead treating all students as if they were from a mainstream Anglo background.

The district's response to the challenges has been to increase expulsions, especially among African American students, and to hand over decisions about programs to the individual schools. The results of the latter policy are mixed. Although a couple of schools showed commitment to multicultural forms of education, most schools ducked the issue.

As reported in Chapter 4, Fresno has grown far too rapidly during the past decade to provide the necessary infrastructure of facilities, programs, and services to accommodate the newcomers. But perhaps more important for understanding this case, we can see in this community how a traditional, unyielding power structure can shackle a school district. Change is not brought about merely because members of an ethnic minority occupy some strategic positions. One third of the Fresno school board is Hispanic, about proportional to their representation in the community. Further, several Hispanics are in key administrative slots. But the crucial factor is that the Anglo community has retained its grip and denies the need for change.

The Fresno case once again reminds us of the important role community history can play in shaping a district. The board has inherited a financial mess that is consuming much of its time and energy. Minority members cannot make their influence felt in program areas when the board is unable or unwilling to put such matters on the agenda.

The case also offers another example of the precarious effects of decentralization. The results of laissez-faire are unpredictable and chaotic; students are left to the mercy of chance. If they happen to attend a school with sensitive and visionary administrators and teachers, they may benefit. But if they are unfortunate enough to be in another kind of school, they lose.

**Mountain View.** In this middle-size district in the San Gabriel Valley east of Los Angeles (8,800 students), about 30% of the students are on AFDC and nearly all receive free lunch. School enrollments increased by one third over the past decade. The percentage of minorities has not changed much in the last decade, but the percentage of limited-English-proficient children has increased, along with the number of immigrants. Most parents do not speak English.

The school board is predominately Anglo. One reason for this is that many families in the district are immigrants without voting rights. Several new board members were elected in the past few years. Currently, only one board member, a Hispanic, supports the superintendent's programs. By most reports, most of the board, and especially the new president, do not cooperate with him.

The superintendent is a Hispanic who had been in office 4 years at the time of our visit. After our site visit, he was replaced before his contract ran out. The teachers' union, which is composed largely of Anglos, supports the board. A major point of contention concerns expulsions, which declined by 50% in the past year. Newer board members want to increase suspensions and expulsions for drugs, weapons, and other offenses, whereas the superintendent demurs.

Several top administrators had been in the district for many years. They seemed to work well together as a team and were supportive of the superintendent. However, they were critical of the board, which in their view was in a power struggle with the superintendent. Despite reports to the contrary, they maintained there was no real gang problem.

The district works closely with community agencies in several efforts in the area of health and programs specifically for students at risk. Most communications with parents are written in both English and Spanish. Some parents participate in committees, but not a large number are involved.

Over the past 18 years, the district has had two Hispanic superintendents (the superintendent at the time of our visit and his predecessor) who have been supportive of bilingual education. Consequently, there is a large, relatively sophisticated bilingual Spanish program for nearly all subject areas; Asians are served with an ESL component. In the primary grades, many classes are conducted primarily in Spanish. Students are gradually moved into regular programs at the end of the third grade.

About half the teachers are Anglo; 40% are Hispanic, 10% Asian and Black. During the past 5 years, the number of bilingual teachers has increased substantially; currently one out of every two is certified for bilingual work. Bilingual-certified teachers receive an additional stipend. Also, part-time bilingual aides are available for most elementary-level classes. There is an extensive in-service program for teachers, and the district provides well-developed curriculum guides.

The schools are generally very supportive of multiculturalism. In recent years, the basic-skills component has become less central than it once was. Teachers are described as dedicated and caring, but they seldom communicate with one another, and they complain about parent apathy. They group students by English-ability levels in subjects such as math and reading, but schools do not place students in tracks. There is little cross-age teaching or tutoring. Students seem to be well treated by teachers, administrators, and school staff. They are given recognition for achievement and attendance. However, in contrast to elementary school teachers, teachers at the intermediate school seem to be less tolerant of students who openly speak their native languages, and they enforce discipline more strictly.

It should be noted that although average test scores declined over the decade, in the first three grades reading scores remained stable or declined only slightly, whereas math scores increased slightly. It is probably no coincidence that the bilingual program has been operating more effectively in those grades.

Mountain View is not overwhelmed by its challenges. There is good support for the schools. Yet, despite strides the district has made toward providing a solid multicultural and bilingual program over the past two decades, it has not been successful in increasing test scores for all students. There has been ample time to cope with the problems, but a formerly receptive response has turned sour.

To solve the district's problems, the new Anglo board members propose getting rid of the troublemakers rather than dealing with root causes.

They were not supportive of the superintendent's program. The case clearly demonstrates that, although a superintendent's priorities can be crucial in the right context, they can be blunted by an unsupportive school board. Even though the superintendent was Hispanic and had a popular Hispanic predecessor, the interests of the Hispanic community were not well represented on the board. The board, in turn, decided to withdraw its support of the superintendent's sympathetic approaches.

**San Gabriel.** One of the oldest school districts in California, San Gabriel has remained small (3,500 students). The population is equally divided among Hispanics, Asians, and Anglos. Hispanics have long been a large part of the surrounding area. For the most part they have remained isolated in the vicinity of one school, the oldest facility in the district. The past 7 years have brought a dramatic increase in Asian families, who were not present in large numbers until recently.

This community has been run by wealthy, politically conservative Anglos for 50 years. The school board has been very supportive of the administration, particularly in the area of staff development. The superintendent is an Anglo male who has held the position for 7 years. Administrators, who often put in very long working days, are accessible to school personnel and considered visionary about program development and implementation. The administration is striving to build a staff that reflects the ethnic diversity of the community, although the pool of credentialed Asians, in particular, is small. Administrators are aware of and concerned about the number of hate crimes in the area and are instituting policies to inhibit such practices. However, they anticipate more racial tension when a new high school becomes a reality and all types of students mix within it.

The administration, which includes several former resource and special education teachers, views cultural diversity as an asset—a challenge for the schools rather than a problem. Over the past few years a generous number of days available for in-service have been devoted to second-language acquisition and multicultural awareness. In addition, the San Gabriel district has been working with the PTA to increase the level of participation among all ethnic groups. Members of the community are represented on several key committees, although the committees are still dominated by Anglos. Every school in the district has a school improvement plan that includes a multicultural component.

The district has always supported bilingual education because of the historic presence of the Hispanic community. This history has predisposed the district to respond in positive ways to the recent influx of non-English-speaking students from countries other than Mexico. Teachers are accustomed to working with non-English-speaking students. However, the huge and disparate influx of students from different cultures has minimized schools' ability to serve all students in bilingual programs. Although one school with a high concentration of Hispanic students has bilingual programs, other schools with greater ethnic diversity are more likely to use sheltered classrooms for non-English-speakers. Moreover, there is some contention within the community about the value of bilingual approaches. The Asian population is especially adamant that children should learn English as soon as possible without the benefit of transition programs. On the other hand, some people believe that both students and parents need help in developing survival language skills.

In the San Gabriel schools, special activities have been designed to encourage participation by all students. All of the teachers interviewed expressed positive attitudes toward the administration and school board. Overall morale was high, but some teachers expressed dismay and frustration at not being able to accomplish more. Their approach to problems was to try different things until they hit upon something that worked.

San Gabriel is an anomaly. In many respects, it does not fit the expected profile for a low performer, given the posited ideal type. Even though its test scores have declined, its efforts and programs are closer to those characteristic of a district with improving test scores. It is small, and the board and superintendent are mutually supportive. It has a long history of working effectively with language minorities and sees the influx of new minorities as enriching and a challenge to be met through language programs and community outreach.

However, underlying these programmatic efforts is a traditional, conservative, Anglo power structure. Moreover, the Hispanic community is of longstanding in the district and has remained sequestered in one neighborhood. Therefore, San Gabriel has not had to confront challenges from new immigrant minorities over the past 15 years, as have some other sites in this study. This relative stability and lack of urgency for innovation may have had some influence on declining test scores.

Another reason for the paradox in the discrepancy between district characteristics and student test scores could lie in differential district testing policies, which are discussed more thoroughly in Chapter 2. San Gabriel, along with Fresno and Rosemead, tested the highest percentage of LEP students in 1989–90: 87%. Generally, the more LEP students tested, the lower the average scores on English tests. Also, assessments are not available in all languages, so not all students can take them. As suggested in Chapter 2, minority and socioeconomic composition might be other factors to consider. More than two thirds of San Gabriel's students are minority, but only 15% of all its students live in poverty (the lowest percentage in the sample). The large number of children from highly educated, middle-class families undoubtedly influences the achievement outcomes.

However, the crucial factor may be reverberations from the rapid influx of such a variety of new language groups. The district is having difficulty extending its traditional bilingual Spanish programs to so many other language groups. Programs must be watered down as they are extended over a wider range of language minorities, and credentialed teachers are not available. Moreover, many Asian parents do not subscribe to the assumptions underlying some bilingual programs employed for Hispanic students. In short, San Gabriel illustrates how even the best intentioned and experienced district can be overwhelmed when confronted by dramatic increases in the variety of languages and associated problems it must cope with.

## CONCLUSIONS

Taken as a whole, these eight cases illustrate that no one overriding feature can account for whether a school district will welcome and successfully meet the challenges of educating the new language minorities now flooding many school districts in the Southwest. However, the patterns do suggest that perhaps a constellation of critical attributes exists and that these, when operating in concert, can tip the balance. They include the following:

- A community not divided by rancorous dissension.
- A cohesive, unified school board that consistently supports the superintendent's programs.
- Fair representation of the dominant minorities on the school board.
- No distracting major financial or political issues to deflect the school board's attention from the challenges of helping newcomers.
- Only one or two non-English-speaking groups, who move in gradually over a period of 5 or 10 years.
- Consensus between the board and the superintendent on the priority of providing programs to help language minorities, and devoted commitment on the part of the superintendent to steadfastly promote this priority throughout the district.
- Firm and vigorous control by the superintendent over key decisions that foster this priority, including administrative appointments and hiring teachers.

When all these factors converge, a district seems to have more success in improving test scores than when the opposite conditions prevail. In particular, in decentralized districts where each school is responsible for finding its own solutions, the district is likely to flounder. The achievements of some schools are frequently undermined by the failures of others. Moreover, teachers and principals do not have the benefit of the powerful incentives and strategic resources commanded by the central administration to support district priorities.

In addition to the attributes listed above, a superintendent who thoroughly understands the community and the minorities represented is a great asset, although this person's ethnic background is not the crucial consideration. In one case a Hispanic superintendent slighted immigrants because he was so close to the traditional Hispanic community. In another, an Anglo woman led a district to successful reforms. In still another, the progressive efforts of a Hispanic superintendent were blocked by a conservative Anglo board.

Another factor that influences success is turnover among principals and teachers; new appointments give a superintendent an opportunity to recruit people who are dedicated to the district's priorities. Successful superintendents also associate with influential community groups, promote outreach programs for parents, and concentrate on obtaining outside funds to support programs. Again, however, none of these elements count unless the superintendent and key staff members are dedicated to the major priority of helping language minorities.

Although most of our cases are consistent with the conclusions just described, there were some anomalies. How to account for the deviant cases is unclear: Perhaps some districts are so overwhelmed by change that there is no way they can successfully cope; perhaps the test score results can be explained by exceptional performance by a particular group; or perhaps such districts do constitute real exceptions that challenge the proposed ideal type.

Figure 5.1 summarizes what we have learned from the case comparisons about the organizational attributes of the high-performing districts. Attributes pertaining to educational and health and human service programs are discussed in Chapter 6.

## Figure 5.1 Attributes of High-Performing Districts

### Community Characteristics

- Community support for schools (e.g., bond issues are generally passed)
- Family atmosphere in the community (i.e., participation, communication interaction, absence of strife)
- Relatively few languages represented
- Population influx took place over a decade (vs. 1 or 2 years)
- Neighborhoods not highly segregated by ethnicity
- Ethnic tensions absent
- Parent committees not dominated by Anglos
- Parents not totally overwhelmed by lack of English skills, economic problems
- Parents not regarded or treated as being apathetic
- Shared power: Community not totally dominated by a single group
- Parents work at school in paid or unpaid jobs
- History of accommodating language minority groups

### School Board Attributes

- Recent arrivals, as well as traditional segments of the community, represented on the board
- Are not all Anglo
- Are not accused of being "politicized," i.e., showing favoritism to particular individuals
- Support the superintendent's priorities and programs
- Are not highly critical of teachers, principals, or the superintendent
- Make regular visits to schools
- Know names of principals, some teachers and parents
- Do not see influxes of new students as an invasion
- Not worried about losing control of the district
- No major rift among board members or with superintendent
- Support an assimilation philosophy
- Have given superintendent a mandate to change the district

### Attributes of the Superintendent

*Personal Characteristics*

- Works long hours
- Not threatened by the presence of problematic students (vs. fear of losing control)
- Informed, visionary, risk taking
- Widely regarded as competent
- Acknowledges and is concerned about social, cultural, and language problems (vs. denial or concern about public relations image)

*Status Characteristics*

- Grew up in or near the district
- Non-Anglo ethnic background
- Views cultural diversity as a strength (vs. a threat or invasion)
- Holds helping disadvantaged, at-risk students as a top priority
- Holds equity and nondiscrimination as top priorities

**Figure 5.1,** *continued*

- Is aggressively trying to build a multi-ethnic, bilingual staff; hiring teachers with bilingual skills is a top priority
- Not only stresses the need of students to learn English, but provides programs for them
- Has successfully reallocated resources within the budget to meet instructional and equity priorities
- Firm minded and determined to implement programs

*Relationships*

- Is accessible and receptive to parents and teachers (vs. detached, noncommunicative)
- Works closely with community leaders
- Has close, collaborative relationships with the board
- Has close ties with recent arrivals in the community (vs. traditional power structure)
- Takes responsibility for interviewing all new teachers and staff
- Handpicks principals
- Works with outside agencies, such as social workers and colleges
- Is very aggressive and successful in obtaining outside funds
- Develops mechanisms to facilitate communication between the central office, schools, and the community

## Attributes of Other Administrators

- Some work long hours
- Not openly critical of the superintendent
- At least one acts as a strong advocate of the bilingual program and other students at risk
- Work as a team : good communication, close, collaborative relationships
- Have a consensus on priorities (goals)

## Authority and the Incentive System

- District is relatively small
- Superintendent controls decisions pertaining to district priorities, but decentralizes many other decisions provided priorities are supported
- District has lean, simple staffing pattern (relatively few administrators)
- Principals are expected to be active in the community and frequently work with parents
- Principals have unwavering commitment to bilingual education and give top priority to hiring bilingual teachers
- Principals are visible throughout the school and intensely involved in daily affairs of their schools (vs. in spending much time in the office)
- Site-level decision makers are not left entirely on their own, but given incentives to give priority to bilingual, disadvantaged children (vs. laissez-faire)
- Bonuses are paid for bilingual certification
- Staff development for teachers is a high priority (vs. made available when teachers request it)
- District programs are supported with follow-through resources and guidance
- Social and educational problems, such as drugs, gangs, and language handicaps, are acknowledged and addressed forcefully
- Previous superintendent(s) were popular and supported by the board
- Previous administrations were innovative

# 6
# Vital Health and
# Human Services

This chapter examines and compares the various service programs supported by the 11 sampled school districts. Our objective is to gauge whether districts classified as high performers, stable performers, and low performers provide different types of service programs. Stable and low performers are considered together, as they exhibit similar patterns. We examine three types of programs in detail—social services, health services, and psychological services—and follow with an analysis of other service programs intended to enhance the life and growth of children and their families.

Our assumption in collecting these data was that the quality of treatment of disadvantaged newcomers within a district and its schools depends not only upon educational programs but also upon how instruction itself interacts with noneducational services. Such services can nurture and sustain well-being and thus contribute substantially to cognitive development.

In the early 1990s, the California State Department of Education (1992) released a report of a task force on coordinated services. We share the department's view that children "have physical and emotional security needs that must be met before they are free to concern themselves with anything else, including doing well in school" (p.87). However, there is no clear consensus on how best to organize services, that is, where and under whose auspices. One common view is that meeting these needs is the obligation of the family and nonschool agencies. Another is that schools are the ideal place to meet a very wide range of these needs. A third view holds that coordinated linkage between schools, families, and other agencies offers the best solution.

In school districts impacted by very large numbers of severely disadvantaged newcomers, this policy question persists, to be sure. Few within such districts nowadays will disagree with the proposition that public schools are of necessity involved in the task of meeting a wide range of pressing needs that are not related to students' cognitive learning. Showing a conviction that schools are the most logical setting for meeting student needs, the California Department of Education (1992) adopted a "philosophy of risk prevention and a vision of the schools as a hub for a coordinated multi-agency response" (p. 87).

We believe that the school district should have a greater role than the community in coordinating health services. However, it is not clear whether strong district activity in coordination of services can mitigate severe community problems. Local, state, and federal agencies as well as philanthropic organizations give funding to a wide variety of agencies whose service programs for children and youth are seldom coordinated or integrated with one another. Therefore, schools have the challenge of harnessing and enhancing the quality of existing programs and linking these programs with the school lives of students.

A number of programs nationwide are beginning to adopt holistic approaches to the needs of children. The U.S. Administration for Children, Youth and Family awarded 32 grants in 1992 for 3- to 5-year demonstration projects. These projects are designed to develop collaborative strategies that would strengthen the connection between Head Start services to children and parents and extend them into the primary grades. The goal is to provide continuity and comprehensiveness in the delivery of a wide range of services that go beyond academic instruction (Jang & Mangione, 1993).

California's Senate Bill 620, the Healthy Start Support Services for Children Act (1993), is an example of an effort made by a state to support and encourage early prevention and intervention programs for children. The goal of this initiative parallels the goal of similar federal programs: to establish a comprehensive statewide system of school-linked services for children and their families, based on the belief that the school is the best setting for coordination.

At the local level, one of the more prominent efforts is being undertaken by Los Angeles Unified School District. As part of the community consensus developed by over 600 community representatives, the district has created a Social Services Council at the district level with counterpart units in subunits and individual schools in order to strengthen collaboration between schools, public service agencies, and private organizations.

The purpose of this chapter is to describe the approaches being taken in our sampled districts, to compare and contrast these, and to relate them to the achievement gain scores that are central to this project. The focus is on identifying successful strategies and promising programs. To assist the reader, Tables 6.1, 6.2, and 6.3 at the end of the chapter display summaries of the extent and levels of service programs in high-performing, stable, and low-performing districts.

## SOCIAL SERVICE PROGRAMS

Central and pivotal as school life may be, children in the Far West spend fewer than one fifth of their hours each week in school during the school year. Those who are not in year-round school have another 3 months without school contact. This out-of-school time brings children and youth into contact with many other social institutions and agencies within their communities. We asked many questions during our field research about how district school staff related to those agencies.

### High-Performing Disticts

In high-performing districts, school–community collaboration is very harmonious, continuous, and supportive. Public schools are generally treated as integral to their communities, and collaboration between agencies across the communities is extensive and deep. Community officials, school administrators, teachers, and parents assert that they enjoy a sense of togetherness in their shared commitment to help children develop to the fullest cognitive, emotional, social, and physical potential. For the most part, our informants in these districts did not report divisions or tensions along racial, ethnic, or other lines.

High-performing districts tend to maintain close working relationships with social workers and the police. A strong police presence is apparent. School-district staff members are alert to needs and danger spots, which generates a stance of anticipation and prevention. Hence various preventive programs are provided by the community and by businesses for students, with special emphasis on personal safety practices and the building of self-esteem. In addition, day-care services are frequently offered.

For example, the Isaac School District provides hot breakfasts and coordinates clothing and school-equipment donations from retirement communities in the surrounding county. Retirees bring in great quantities of clothing, help prepare it for use, and stay on to mingle with and share in the lives of the primary schoolchildren. Isaac schools also have strong safety and security operations and exercise strict disciplinary control, particularly at the junior high school, in order to prevent the penetration of drug and gang operations. A police officer works in the junior high school full time.

In California, Rosemead's surrounding area, like the neighborhood surrounding Isaac in Arizona, is experiencing the widespread influence of gang recruitment, gang fights, and drug trafficking. During each successive year of the 1980s, more babies were born with prenatal addictions to several types of narcotics, and the number of neglected and abused children increased each year. A school social worker who receives many referrals from principals, nurses, and teachers through a communitywide hot line feels that Rosemead badly needs its own police department in order to meet rising numbers of crime incidents, although she and others also commend some members of the county sheriff's office who have done their best to help schoolchildren. Several respondents, for instance, spoke admiringly of a dedicated Hispanic woman, a deputy sheriff, who visits schools and classrooms regularly and conducts discussion sessions with students on how to avoid drug use and how to build self-esteem. The Rosemead schools have also recently instituted a dress code intended to prevent symbolic displays of gang colors and articles of clothing.

The National public schools enjoy strong support and cooperation from the city's mayor, city council members, and officers of the Chamber of Commerce. Our evidence suggests that these officials collaborate very effectively with the superintendent and principals, and they, in turn, are in close communication with the police, fire, and other departments of the city government.

National's city government funds a full-time police presence in the schools, and an officer regularly conducts the DARE drug education program. The police and a community service clinic work in tandem with the district administration at trying to prevent and to control gang violence and drug trafficking. The National School District and its schools sponsor the Juveniles Out of Gangs (JOG) program—a drug-prevention project involving fifth graders. Students and parents participate in antidrug conferences, classes, and an after-school club run by a teacher. National's school administrators also work with the local government to establish what they call "drug-free zones" around schools, areas with a radius of 1,000 yards that are patrolled as a protection against drug use or dealing. City and police officials also express pride in their agencies' efforts to improve minority group representation in their work forces.

## Stable and Low-Performing Districts

Districts that showed little or no change in achievement scores offered only very limited social services in the schools or through community agencies. We do not think this situation can be accounted for by limited resources. Rather, the communities served by these districts show political factionalism and racial/ethnic tensions separating groups within them, with a resulting lack of concern about the needs of ethnic and language minority newcomers. In addition, little cooperation is apparent between the police department, social workers, and the schools. A few business-sponsored programs may exist, but only limited day care is available.

For instance, in Balsz, near Phoenix, a social worker spends 1 day a week in the schools and 4 days a week in other public districts in the county. Occasionally she works with the district's school psychologist, and the two of them might visit a student's home. State police officers make an annual presentation to each school on issues related to youth gangs. The district also sponsors a confidential drug-dependency support program that makes referrals for children from homes with chemically dependent family members. Teachers involved in this program are given in-service training to equip them to cooperate with family members. Balsz also operates a day-care center that requires most families to pay for services. Some local businesses donate funds to Balsz schools for special purposes such as summer jobs for youth. However, the activities we have described are very limited.

Like stable districts, districts whose test scores deteriorated also suffer from racial and intergroup tensions grounded in mutual distrust. For the most part, these districts and their corresponding communities have not made the investments needed to mount and maintain social services adequate to ameliorate the difficulties faced by disadvantaged students. Relations between social workers and school staff are unclear, strained at times, or nonexistent, and social workers are pessimistic about meeting the needs of children and their families in these communities. However, several of the low-performing districts have one or two distinctive programs to provide children and youth with social services of a limited kind.

The low performers all acknowledge long-standing problems with gangs yet have made few organized attempts to deal with them, instead either ignoring or deemphasizing these problems. For example, Sunnyside district staff members report severe gang activity in and around their campuses, but we observed little action by them or their community leaders to control gangs. Every year sixth graders are shown a half-hour film on gang prevention, but the schools lack security officers and gang protection procedures. One security guard is assigned to protect the 1,200 students in the junior high school.

San Gabriel shows some concern over the increasing frequency and severity of crimes committed on campuses. The district has implemented security measures to control crimes after a teacher was assaulted on a campus. Visitors to San Gabriel schools are required to wear passes from the district office before they enter a campus, and a dress code is enforced to discourage students from flaunting gang colors and other clothing symbols. These efforts are not sufficient to prevent the crimes that occur almost daily, however.

Unlike the other low performers, Mountain View has close ties between city, county, and school health and social service agencies. The community is supportive of its public school and concerned about the safety and well-being of all children. Several programs are in operation to prevent students from becoming involved with drugs, alcohol, or gangs, for example. The police work cooperatively with Mountain View's school staff and students and contribute effectively to workshops and training about drugs and alcohol, truancy, and child abuse. Students also get opportunities to take internships in local businesses. In addition, the health center provides work experience to selected students for 10 weeks under a program designed to motivate at-risk students and to get them out of harmful situations.

As we have noted elsewhere, Fresno is one of the poorest metro areas in the nation, a determination based on the number of families living below the federal poverty level and the number receiving AFDC. Although many children in Fresno suffer from various forms of abuse and neglect, the city offers no child-abuse prevention programs, except for a hot line to report the severest cases. In addition, the city experienced rising crime and delinquency rates during the 1980s, at levels that exacerbated tensions between the diverse ethnic subcommunities. School staffs report that they lack the resources to address student needs, and they express skepticism about their ability to help. Social workers report that they get very few referrals from the schools, and those they do receive are limited to conditions that are mandated under law to require reporting. However, they do sometimes receive calls from school staff asking them to help present in-service training sessions on child protective service policies and practices. There is an effort within the Fresno School District to provide translators during community meetings with language minority newcomers and their families.

## HEALTH AND HUMAN SERVICE PROGRAMS

Nutrition and the physical well-being of children should be a primary concern for educators. Hungry, weak, and ill children cannot learn to their fullest potential. In the United States, about 20% of children live in poverty (Wright, 1996), one of the highest poverty rates in the world's industrialized countries.

Because of severe budgetary reductions and a general lack of resources, many school districts and communities are experiencing difficulties in providing necessary services and programs to children and families. More doctors, nurses, counselors, and therapists are needed. Home, school, and community should be partners and share responsibility to ensure that all children and families in need are receiving proper services and treatment.

Health agencies should have translators available or hire bilingual staff to help families who have difficulty communicating in English. A positive attitude, commitment, and concern from schools and health service providers can greatly enhance the quality of services available to children and their families. A few patterns emerge as the school districts are viewed in light of the three types of achievement change.

## High-Performing Districts

The high-performing school districts and their communities overall have many programs and health services available to families and emphasize children's well-being. In general, good cooperation and communication between teachers and health service providers also characterize these school districts. Local health agencies and health providers demonstrate sensitivity and recognize the importance of providing health services to all the children and families in need, including the multilingual minority population. Some of the services often provided by high-performing districts are free immunizations, presentations on health issues, referrals to health agencies, health education programs, provision of bilingual staff in clinics, and translator programs. We conclude that high-performing districts are more innovative and more cooperative; they have clearly established goals for their children and therefore proceed to establish stable and long-term efforts with local health agencies and the community.

Some examples of services provided by high-performing districts follow. Rosemead has a paramedic squad to respond to emergency situations. The city has two mental health hospitals, three medical centers, and two county health clinics in nearby cities. A team called the Refugee Assistance program provides translators to help Asian families in one of the health clinics. The clinic has several Asian and Filipino nurses who also serve as translators if needed. The local medical center receives referrals from a school nurse regarding immunizations. The school nurse and health providers in the community communicate well and work collaboratively. They meet every year to discuss issues relating to immunization and TB screening, and children are immunized before entering school through the Back to School Rush Program. One medical center in the community is the district's partner in funding a new physical education curriculum. Through a grant, Rosemead was able to provide in-service training for staff, establish an indoor fitness program, and provide access to a consultation hot line.

In the National School District, the community health clinic (staffed by three doctors, two of them pediatricians, and one physician assistant) provides services to families and children. It has its own pharmacy laboratory. All the staff members at the health clinic are bilingual, so Hispanic and Filipino parents who do not speak English are easily served in Spanish or Tagalog. The members of the clinic give presentations on adolescent health to schools and provide one-on-one counseling for children who are obese. The clinic sends flyers once a year to the community to make sure that children are getting their immunizations and provides general physicals for sports activities. The clinic also provides free immunizations and various screenings such as hearing, vision, and blood pressure to families and children in the community.

## Stable and Low-Performing School Districts

Stable districts offer limited health care, and medical services are generally nonexistent in low-performing school districts. This is certainly a consequence of the community's attitude and history in these districts. Because schools and districts generally cannot provide comprehensive health services to children and families, an alternative is to establish ongoing and mutually supportive efforts with community health agencies. As evidenced by the dearth of social services, the stable districts and especially the low-performing districts have failed to integrate themselves into the social fabric of the community and to establish cooperative links with other agencies. Mountain View is an exception in this regard, and its position in the low-performing category could be the result of other confounding factors.

A lack of primary medical care and providers in the Washoe County community has made it difficult for families to receive health care. Many of them have neither a health plan nor Medicare. Two school nurses spend 1 or 2 days a week at each school, and a health aide helps with routine first aid. Immunization is available through the county clinic. The Washoe County Medical Center works with the schools to help students who are interested in health careers.

However, the community is making some efforts to improve services to children and families. Over the past 6 years, through a private comprehensive nonprofit organization called the Children's Cabinet, which involves public officials and business leaders, Washoe County has attempted to address its children's needs and to fill in the gaps between existing services to its children. Its health services include a teen clinic that offers pregnancy testing and counseling, birth control, and general checkups. A child's shelter and companion teenage shelter were built recently. Efforts in the nonprofit organization also include prevention, mainstreaming, and coordination of existing services to facilitate and improve access for families in need, and the development of additional services for children and families on the basis of documented community needs. The Children's Cabinet also established an independent Family Resource Center. Although the Children's Cabinet is an exemplary program, it can help only a small percentage of the children in need.

Families and children in San Gabriel are provided health services and counseling through three community medical, family, and health centers. Community members at Sunnyside pay whatever they can afford for basic health services offered through the mobile health clinic. Mountain View has a primary prevention program in grades K–3, which includes physical exams for all incoming kindergartners. A nurse and health aide provide services to the schools, and a few volunteer teachers are involved in the immunization program so that mothers can get their toddlers immunized. A health coordinator in the district works with the health clinic in the city, and families who do not speak English are served through an interpreter program in the clinic.

In spite of Fresno's large enrollment increase over the last decade, the number of school nurses has remained static. Thus nurses in the district provide only limited mandated services to the children, such as hearing examinations. Health education programs for children and families are lacking, even though many health problems (such as a very high rate of teen pregnancy) exist. There is also a lack of communication and coop- eration between the schools and the county health clinic; the clinic gets few referrals from the schools. However, the clinic is making a limited outreach effort to the schools. Its staff provides immunizations and physi- cals to schoolchildren, gives presentations, and participates in health fairs. The clinic has a small bilingual staff for the Hispanic population but none for the Southeast Asian population. The poor and minority populations in the community do not get proper and necessary medical services. A good indication of this deteriorating situation is the general shortage of health professionals in the area and the increasing unwillingness of doctors to accept Medi-Cal patients.

## PSYCHOLOGICAL SERVICE PROGRAMS

Disadvantaged newcomers are often in extreme need of help with the emotional and psychological stresses generated in their daily lives. Accord- ingly, it is important to note that family policies and issues of family well- being are powerfully affected by resource allocations from federal, state, and local governments (Zimmerman, 1992). The lack of a clear set of pri- orities and policies at all levels has left many school districts uncertain about how to provide psychological services to students.

The main difference we observed among districts in providing psychological counseling services was in the amount and effectiveness of the services available to meet the needs of students who actively seek help, especially concerning problems with gangs, drugs, alcohol, and abuse. In most of the school districts we visited, staff complained about insufficient counseling time and too few psychologists.

## High-Performing Districts

In school districts with improving test scores, more extensive counseling services and programs are available than in low-performing districts. Various community organizations are involved with schools and help in improving psychological counseling services to children and their families. Self-esteem and counseling programs are available, and mechanisms for resolving conflict are evident.

In the high-performing school districts, adults treat students with care, respect, affection, and attention. Students are cheerful, enthusiastic about being in school, and generally feel safe there. Isaac focuses on the equitable and sensitive treatment of children. When fights and quarrels occur among students, adults immediately intervene to prevent their escalation. Students discuss interpersonal problems and seek guidance freely. Peer counseling is available, and social trust is high. Isaac also maintains two full-time psychologists who work with children from all elementary schools on an individual basis and in long-term group sessions. They also refer students and parents to other mental health agencies.

Rosemead has several community counseling agencies working with the district free of charge and has increased the number of counselors and psychologists to meet the needs of its students. Four psychologists, who demonstrate a positive attitude toward changes taking place in the schools and the community, provide services to five schools. One bilingual counselor also helps primarily Hispanic students. Different community organizations offer counseling and family education classes. The Asian Pacific Counseling and the Asian Youth Counseling Centers provide counseling and homework assistance to the district's Asian population. Another project, the Juvenile Diversion Program, helps students build self-esteem, provides counseling, and plans lessons once a week to help students avoid getting involved with gangs. At Rosemead, some racial tensions among children are evidenced by name calling, but these tensions are usually resolved by teachers and counselors through discussions and lessons.

The school psychologist in the National School District assists students in testing and counseling; consults with school personnel and parents regarding children with learning, social, behavioral, and/or emotional difficulties; and makes recommendations for intervention. The teachers and the psychologist communicate and cooperate well with each other. The psychologist gets referrals from teachers about drug-related abuse and often receives phone calls at night from teachers who are concerned about children with problems related to drug and gang issues. The school psychologist also serves as a liaison between the school and other school-related community services and agencies, and coordinates the delivery of service for children requiring psychological intervention. One community agency is providing counselors and translators to schools with children from Asian communities.

## Stable and Low-Performing Districts

To some degree, school districts whose test scores have remained stable are working cooperatively with their communities and the different service agencies to provide psychological services to families and children. These include counseling programs, motivational talks, and referrals to agencies. Lines of communication between psychologists and teachers are open.

This is especially so in the Washoe School District. A central referral team, consisting of members from different community agencies, provides services in referral and family counseling and coordinates needed services for children and families. The police department cooperates with school attendance officers on truancy cases. The School Early Intervention program assists elementary school children and their families through counseling, liaison and coordination of services, and parenting classes. Ten school psychologists in Washoe do testing, provide some counseling, and consult with school personnel and parents regarding children. A school counselor serves as the case manager for special education referrals, reports child abuse, and consults with teachers and parents. This person also provides individual, small-group, and large-group counseling and conducts parent classes.

Balsz has a school psychologist who makes referrals to social workers and follows up with home visits to troubled families in the company of a social worker or an ESL teacher. The school psychologist also works with the special education teachers and tries to help children with emotional or learning disability problems. Students receive counseling through the school counseling program, which is funded through federal drug programs. The majority of the issues dealt with are related to dysfunctional homes and traumas such as the imprisonment of a parent or a sibling. To motivate children, role models and professionals are invited from the community to give talks to the students.

School districts whose test scores deteriorated generally lack counselors and psychologists to meet the growing needs of students and their families. Few community agencies are working with schools to provide counseling services. The efforts made by these school districts are minimal at best. One problem is the lack of coordination, integration, and support among various stakeholders.

Concern over a number of hate-crime incidents among students and communities is growing, and more and more students are carrying guns and knives to school. However, low-performing districts generally do not have a hate-crime policy. Mechanisms for resolving these incidents are very limited, and no counseling or parent education on these issues is provided at the school and community level, even though the community and the district acknowledge that racial tensions between different ethnic groups will likely escalate.

As an example of the limitations in low-performing districts, a licensed clinical social worker in Fresno spends only 8 hours a week counseling students with emotional problems. In Sunnyside, a half-time, school-based elementary counselor works with children who come from broken, abusive, and violent family backgrounds to prevent behavior problems. In addition, the counselor resolves conflicts and conducts sessions for teachers. The police department in Mountain View offers a counseling program to families with problems such as drug abuse. However, very few slots are available for appointments, and families are often placed on a long waiting list.

The behavior problems of students in Fresno are treated differently from those exhibited by students in high-performing districts. More minority students than White students are expelled, and teachers refer more minority students for suspension or expulsion. Many of the teachers are ignorant about their students' backgrounds, unlike the teachers in high-performing school districts who often know their students by their first names. The school board and upper level administrators may be aware of this situation but choose to disregard it.

## OTHER SERVICE PROGRAMS

Although programs to address social, health, and psychological problems are the major concern of school districts, other types of service programs with less immediate impact are nonetheless important. These programs are often preventive and nurturing in nature, serving to build long-term structural improvement and goodwill among key constituents in a district, such as school personnel, community members, and parents.

Educational programs, English courses for parents, communication and translation assistance, cultural programs to recognize diversity, and park and recreation programs are examples of such services that help to weave a fabric of richness in a district (Harry, 1992). Rather than being contingent upon funding resources, many of these programs come from and rely on the commitment of the community and district. Most of the school districts recognize their importance and promote various ways in which the lives of children and their families can be enriched.

## High-Performing Districts

Although all school districts attempt to provide their students with nonacademic activities, these differ greatly in nature and variety. High-performing districts offer more numerous and varied activities and programs to develop children's social skills, self-confidence, and self-esteem. Extracurricular and after-school activities in these school districts abound, including choir, art club, drama club, marching band, drill team, and the Kiwanis Builder's Club (a service club to the school and the community), to name a few.

High performers have good park and recreation programs. For example, the YMCA at National provides many sports and crafts classes to youngsters to get them off the street and keep them out of trouble. Addressing the situation created by an increasing number of latch-key children from single-parent homes, a television program called "Children's Line" on a local channel offers children at home alone the opportunity to call the line and talk to someone. Rosemead has a community center where children participate in activities such as dance and sports. Isaac also shows great enthusiasm for sports, emphasizes physical education, and has a large gymnasium to support its program. Students also participate in activities such as band and choral teams.

There are library programs for children in these communities. The community library at Rosemead operates children's summer reading programs. However, some of the low-performing districts also have library programs; for example, the San Gabriel School District has Friday Readings, a summer reading program for children, and special Saturday events for families.

In addition to activities and programs, districts differ in the degree to which parents are involved in the activities of the schools. Parent involvement and parent education are critical elements in any program whose goal is to enhance children's well-being and success rate. Districts and schools should provide various opportunities for parents to get involved in their children's education. Communication with parents in their native language and in ways that facilitate their input and encourage their participation will contribute to their children's educational process. Most school districts in the study had translators or interpreters available, but not always. The availability of translators for meetings and events was more apparent in the high-performing school districts. These districts were also more likely to have several programs to educate parents about social issues such as gangs, drug, and health.

Isaac provides parents with social, teaching, and learning programs. Adult literacy training, evening instruction for parents desiring a GED, and a variety of cultural events, fairs, and extended field trips for both parents and children are offered. Parents at Rosemead are being educated about gangs through a local drug program. The Parent Taught Program teaches parents of children ages 2 and 3 better parenting skills. Many parents with newborn babies at National are benefiting from a program called Parents As Teachers, which helps them get their children off to the best possible educational start in life. Recognizing that many parents fail to appreciate why children need to be vaccinated, the community also assumes responsibility for educating parents on health issues. The health educator gives presentations and sends out notices to parents about immunization and other health-related matters.

## Stable and Low-Performing Districts

Stable and low-performing districts may offer a few parent education programs or provide limited after-school and extracurricular activities and programs. They may have library programs. However, translators and language assistance for parents with limited English are lacking, and parental involvement is generally low.

School districts whose scores deteriorated offer some events for parents. These include workshops on topics such as self-esteem and drug and alcohol awareness, a health and wellness fair, and an anti-gang information guide. However, in these districts most parents do not get involved with their children's education, and the schools do not have resources to develop programs that respect and accommodate parents' work schedules and provide child care.

In Washoe County, the nonprofit organization (Children's Cabinet) offers parent education classes. Parents are provided with information about different classes, all of which are free—some in Spanish—through a Parent Education Network hot line.

Several after-school programs and extracurricular events are available to the students in these stable school districts. These include sports, band programs, chorus, and special interest clubs. The students' level of participation in such activities at Balsz is high, partly owing to the availability of late busses.

To address the growing problem of teen pregnancy, Sunnyside has the Teen Parenting program, which encourages teen mothers to take courses before and after the birth of their child. Classes with topics such as self-esteem, social development, suicide prevention, substance abuse, and the risk of gang involvement are offered to parents in Mountain View.

In these districts, after-school activities are very limited, sometimes because schools have no means of ensuring the safety of their students after school and while on the way home. Limited funds and resources also sometimes prevent some districts from providing after-school busses. Many parents, even those who own cars, cannot afford to take time out to pick up their children.

A mixed picture is offered by low-performing districts with respect to providing community members with basic facilities. Even though Fresno has experienced a large population increase in the past 15 years, the city has not built any new libraries or community parks since the 1970s. In fact, severe budgetary restrictions forced many of the branch libraries to shut down or greatly reduce their hours. The last community park built in Fresno was in 1978. Since then, the city has grown by 160,000 people, nearly doubling its population. Sunnyside has a park and recreation center where children participate in after-school activities such as sports and crafts, and the center supervises and helps keep children off the street. However, these activities are limited.

## CONCLUSIONS

The common thread running through these school districts and their communities is increasing poverty and family problems—violence, gangs, drugs, alcohol, single parenthood. Communities need many more service programs to meet the needs of their children and families, and they are having a difficult time responding to the increasing demands arising from social, health, and psychological issues. Some do not know how best to respond to the needs of their children, although they recognize the compelling nature of the demand for additional services. Poor economic situations, limited resources, and tight budgets make it harder for them to provide help or improve existing services for children and families. In most cases, schools lack health providers and counselors. Communities need more police officers and social workers and are overcrowded with families who need help in dealing with problems of violence, gangs, drug, and alcohol.

However, even in the face of these pressing challenges, some communities and schools are making a concerted effort to meet the needs of the children and their families. There are places where different ethnic groups and social agencies, recognizing the importance of the children's well-being, cooperate. Many different community agencies and members maintain positive attitudes about the changes taking place in their communities and are working closely with schools and families.

Such districts are trying to control gangs and drug-related activities through various programs that motivate students and promote their self-esteem and self-confidence. These efforts are especially apparent and widespread in high-performing districts. Superintendents, teachers, principals, politicians, and members of different businesses in these districts are more visible and obviously care about their schools and children. Child-abuse, gang, and drug prevention efforts are widespread and are being incorporated into the curriculum and school activities. Various types of health care coverage are provided to the children and their families. Teachers, counselors, and health providers are communicating, coordinating, and cooperating with each other. Children receive counseling services and are treated with respect. Parent education is emphasized and promoted through various programs. Many recreation and sports activities are available for children. Members of different ethnic groups work cooperatively, and little racial and ethnic tension exists.

Stable districts and their communities, on the other hand, do not appear to place as high a priority on providing services to children and families. These communities are less sensitive to the needs of the minority population. Translators are seldom available in meetings with limited-English-speaking parents. Families often have to make an extra effort to receive primary care. For example, a family in one of the school districts we visited had to go to the hospital emergency room for treatment of an ear infection, which could easily have been treated at a clinic or a doctor's office.

In stable districts, some worthy programs exist to serve children and families. Washoe County, for example, has its nonprofit organization to provide social and health services, an exemplary coordinated services agency that is working collaboratively with the school district to move into the schools.

School districts sharing similar demographic characteristics and challenges might benefit by adopting some of the promising programs in stable districts, such as the district service center in Franklin McKinley, which provides comprehensive services for its students and families. As described in Chapter 5, this approach is unique in providing services to children, even though some controversy has arisen in the district about the decision to build the multimillion dollar district center. Although Washoe County and Franklin McKinley are currently in the stable-performer category, the efforts described here may cause their status to rise in the years to come.

A district's ability to provide services is contingent on community support. When racial harmony and cooperation exist among different ethnic subcommunities, it is easier for schools to bring together the needed services to the children and families. Unfortunately, the low-performing districts often suffer from ethnic tension, factionalism, and lack of cooperation among different members of the community, who hold negative attitudes or display insensitivity toward the needs of the minority population. Without a mandate from the community, the public service agencies will not extend themselves to cooperate with a district. Thus many services will be limited or not available to children and families.

In general, low-performing districts have expended very little effort. They either deny problems or lack the vision or commitment necessary to alleviate them. Even when the need for help is recognized, staff members may not know where or how to find it among a complex of agencies with vaguely defined mandates. However, Mountain View offers an exception to this general picture. Perhaps its lack of demonstrable student success is merely time-related; that is, the positive effects of providing services need more time to register.

We found that the amount of resources available (in terms of per pupil expenditures) does not appear to determine improvement in student performance unless accompanied by other things, such as cooperation among ethnic groups, social agencies and schools. Some of the lowest performers had below average per pupil expenditures, and two of the high performers had below average per pupil expenditures. All of the case study districts experienced funding increases during the 1980s, which meant that some extra resources came to all of them. More importantly, the evidence that both school and social service improvements for children and their families will cost more over time than is now being expended is substantial.

The data reviewed in this chapter suggest that there are both quantitative and qualitative differences in the services provided to the children and their families by the high-performing and low-performing school districts (see Tables 6.1, 6.2, and 6.3). Some of the districts in the stable category could be either in transition or simply stagnant, falling between the other two categories because of their lack of capacity or commitment.

**Table 6.1 Summary of Four Types of Service Programs for High-Performing School Districts**

| Social Services | Health Services | Psychological Services | Other Services |
|---|---|---|---|
| • Have close working relationship with social workers, police | • Provide free immunizations and other health-related tests | • Receive support and psychological services from various community counseling agencies | • Emphasize and promote parent education |
| • Provide various preventive gang and drug-related programs | • Enjoy good communication and cooperation between teachers and health service providers | • Provide various counseling services to minority children and their families | • Offer various parent education programs on social issues |
| • Provide child abuse preventive program | • Emphasize children's physical well-being | • Help students to build self-esteem through various counseling programs | • Educate parents on health-related issues |
| • Exercise strict disciplinary control for prevention of gangs and drugs | • Inform communities regarding health-related issues | • Have good communication between teachers and psychologists | • Provide variety of activities and programs for social skills, self-esteem |
| • Have strong social goals | • Give presentations on health issues | • Have a positive attitude and total commitment from school staff | • Have numerous extra-curricular and after-school activities |
| • Have dedicated full-time police officer on campus | • Make referrals to health agencies | • Have mechanism for resolving conflicts | • Supply translators for meetings and events |
| • Show cooperation from teachers, nurses, principals, and social service agencies | • Provide health education programs | • Treat children with respect, affection, and care | • Have good park and recreation programs |
| • Get strong community support and have strong community linkage | • Have bilingual staff in clinics | | • Offer library programs |
| • Display harmony and cooperation among different ethnic groups | • Offer translator programs | | |
| • Have various business-sponsored programs | | | |
| • Provide free and extensive day care services | | | |

**Table 6.2 Summary of Four Types of Service Programs for Stable School Districts**

| Social Services | Health Services | Psychological Services | Other Services |
|---|---|---|---|
| • Exhibit little cooperation between police dept. and the schools | • Have limited health care and lack medical facilities | • Provide counseling programs to children and families | • Have a few parent education programs |
| • Receive minimal social support from the community and community agencies | • Lack cooperation between districts and health agencies | • Receive some cooperation and psychological services from community agencies | • Provide several after-school or extracurricular programs |
| • Show insensitivity to minority/multilingual populations | • Have created different approaches to meet the needs of children | • Provide talks to motivate children | • Lack language assistance and translators for limited-English-speaking parents |
| • Suffer from factionalism and racial tension | • Offer a few health-related education programs | • Show some communication between psychologists and teachers | |
| • Have a few business-sponsored programs | | • Make referrals to few agencies | |
| • Offer limited day care services | | | |

140

**Table 6.3 Summary of Four Types of Service Programs for Low-Performing School Districts**

| Social Services | Health Services | Psychological Services | Other Services |
|---|---|---|---|
| • Have unclear, strained relationships between social workers and the schools | • Provide very limited health services | • Provide limited psychological counseling services | • Offer some health- and social-related events and workshops for parents |
| • Lack social resources to deal with problems | • Show lack of communication and cooperation among health professionals | • Lack counselors and psychologists | • Display low parent involvement |
| • Show insufficient efforts to control crimes and lack police officers | • Supply translators for some minority population groups | • Have no community counseling agencies working with schools | • Provide very limited after-school and extracurricular activities |
| • Make very few referrals to social agencies | • Make very few referrals to health agencies | • Fail to link with and get support from community agencies | • Lack translators |
| • Ignore existing social problems | • Lack health professionals | • Lack coordination, integration and support | • Display mixed pictures in basic community facilities |
| • Hold pessimistic view in solving problems | • Lack health education programs | | • Offer library programs |
| • Display racial tension and distrust | | | |
| • Lack child care services | | | |
| • Have some social support from businesses | | | |

# 7
# Conclusions

This book grew out of a field study that sought to locate, describe, and analyze demographically impacted public school districts in the Far West. The study was based on the hypothesis that some districts responded effectively to the foremost educational challenge of the 1980s, but most did not. We think that challenge consisted of organizing whole districts and schools within them in such a way as to host optimally those we called newcomers—the ethnic and language minority students whose circumstances placed them at extreme risk developmentally and educationally. And we think that challenge remains foremost in the 1990s and will continue into the next century.

We knew that school districts and schools within them differ substantially in their performance in hosting and educating minority newcomers and disadvantaged students. We also knew that at least two more general factors shape the context in which these differences appear. First, the relative affluence or poverty of a community's population is a powerful predictor of the teaching and learning outcomes of public school districts across a universe of communities; we called this the "structural dominance" effect. Second, the racial/ethnic composition of communities—both the proportion of minority households and their combinations—affects instructional performance conditions. And although in this study the percentage of students in poverty and the percentage of minority students were negatively and significantly related to students' average scores on reading and math, poverty and minority status were not significantly related to *change* in achievement over time. Thus change in achievement over time was not predetermined by structural dominance (e.g., by background status variables that are its indicators).

The guiding purpose of the study was not to revisit these generalizations, however, but to locate, identify, and synthesize conceptually the characteristics of communities, school districts, and schools within them that account for their fundamental differences in quality of treatment of learners and in student outcomes. If this could be accomplished, we thought, and if some of the characteristics were amenable to deliberate, planned adoption, then the project would contribute some vital clues to models of performance for use in technical assistance work and in the exchange of knowledge between educational research and practice. The research team sought answers, therefore, to these questions:

- Are there public school districts in the metro West that succeed in educating disadvantaged children and offer authentic models of good practice?
- What combination of factors—organizational, cultural, and pro-grammatic—lead to these models and provide conditions for their feasibility?
- Do successful districts have distinctive features that form a pattern that contrasts with those present in less successful districts?
- Can we devise a kind of ideal type of what works well academically and socially in hosting low-income ethnic and language minority learners, and do the types have heuristic value for other communities and districts?

Keeping in mind the independent influences of income, race, ethnicity, and language, as well as scope and pace of changes in minority enrollments, we organized our inquiry around a series of major intervening variables. These can be summarized as follows:

Metro area communities and their public school districts vary substantially in their historical development and political cultures. State contexts vary greatly in depth of public fiscal investment in education, in proactivity in stimulating school improvement, and in receptivity to multicultural needs and interests. Within those contexts, communities reflect state trends but vary in their own origins, emphases, and practices.

The districts and their schools also vary in their treatment of disadvantaged learners as a function of the ways in which they are organized and how their organization is designed and executed to assist those learners. The districts and their schools vary in the quality with which they design and implement educational and social service programs, and part of this variation will stem from the characteristics, abilities, and working conditions of the teachers and other staff.

In the following sections, we discuss the quantitative and qualitative findings of the study. We then examine their implications for impacted urban districts.

## QUANTITATIVE FINDINGS

Correlations were run for all California metropolitan districts between mean achievement test scores in 1984 and 1989 and five indicators of student disadvantagement status. Results supported the structural dominance hypothesis. The higher the levels of student poverty, limited-English-proficiency, and ethnic minority status, the lower the average achievement scores tended to be. The percentage of minority students in a district in 1989 correlated –.72 with mean achievement scores. The percentage of students with poor English skills correlated –.59 with achievement scores; and percentage of households in poverty correlated –.75 with achievement scores (all of these were significant).

By contrast, the achievement *change scores* (change over time) were not significantly correlated with these independent demographic variables. Change in achievement was not related to status variables, indicating that the structural dominance effect does not hold for change over time. This is reasonable because a district with high poverty in 1980, for instance, would probably yield low absolute mean achievement results in 1984 and would generally repeat that relational pattern in 1989. While the poverty level persisted, however, learning outcomes might have improved, changed very little, or declined relative to 1984.

The percentage of students in poverty was significantly and positively correlated with each of the five scales, as was the percentage of LEP students and the percentage of minority students with four of the scales (excluding Quality of Organization). In other words, quality of school programs (QE), teaching (QT), and human relations(QM and QI) were higher in the most disadvantaged districts. Such districts, with several exceptions, were predictably more likely to become sensitized to issues of multiculturalism, social integration, and the organization of school system services. This heightened sensitivity did not in itself lead to gains in achievement test scores, however.

The performance of districts over time as measured by change in achievement was, in fact, not significantly correlated with any of the five rating scales. Change in achievement correlated about .30 with Quality of Education, Quality of Teaching, and Quality of Integration scales, indicating only a modest relationship between gains in achievement and the general quality of the educational program.

## QUALITATIVE FINDINGS

### Instructional Strategies, Programs, and Teachers

The most distinctive feature of the high-performing districts is a programmatic emphasis on student language development. High-performing districts provide comprehensive second-language programs and resources, supply sufficient primary-language materials, use strict criteria for transitioning students into English, and provide sheltered content classes to small language subgroups. These features were absent in low-performing districts. A core of bilingual teachers constitutes the educational backbone of the best second-language programs.

The great range of particular programs carried on by all of the districts appears to make very little overall difference: It is the quality of implementation and the cooperative integration between the programs that has a marked effect. All of the districts and nearly all of the schools we visited had federal Chapter 1 funds, for example. The high-performing districts use most of those funds to supplement and enrich the core curriculum of the district, which is itself designed to benefit disadvantaged learners. They tend to use schoolwide or after-school Chapter 1 programs rather than the pullout mode. Low-performing districts tend to use Chapter 1 funds to pull slow learners or at-risk students out of their regular classes for brief periods of special enrichment or tutoring and remediation.

The three high-performing districts differ markedly from other districts, not in teacher credentials or pay but in the intensity and quality of the effort expended to recruit and support teachers professionally; in collaborative relations between teachers, parents, and administrators; and in quality of in-service training opportunities. Teachers in the high-performing districts not only are more consistently matched ethnically and by language with their students but also are more likely to be certified bilingual and ESL instructors as well.

In addition, teachers in the high-performing districts display higher, more positive morale; express the belief that they enjoy considerable autonomy within and under the shared goals of their schools and districts; and exhibit higher, more focused energy in the conduct of their work than do their counterparts in other districts. These teachers also communicate high academic expectations to their students; believe all students can learn; recognize and reward their students frequently; and take great pride in their own instructional successes.

The most successful districts provide organizational structures that facilitate the ability of teachers to deliver more effective instruction. These include cooperative learning, peer and cross-grade tutoring and mentoring, equalized access for all students to a core curriculum, flexible grouping methods, and norms opposed to tracking and ability grouping. High-performing districts have a unique focus on teacher collaboration, planning and decision making, using strategies such as site-based management, team teaching, grade-level or subject-matter articulation, and providing opportunities for teachers to work together.

High-performing districts show a common emphasis on certain instructional approaches as well: a focus on meaning, encouraging active student participation, validating multicultural experiences, using manipulatives and realia and a literature-based language-arts program. The aspects that seem to count the most include a strong focus on teacher quality and staff development, an emphasis on teacher collaboration and planning, use of instructional organizational structures that provide opportunities for teachers to deliver effective instruction, and provision of comprehensive second-language programs.

Some of these efforts and approaches were present in low-performing districts, of course. We found that the adoption of the full range of practices is what differentiates between high- and low-performing districts.

## Community History and Culture

All 11 communities and their public schools were chosen for comparative analysis because they were heavily impacted by an influx of ethnic and language minority students during the 1980s and because they differed markedly in their achievement gain scores over those years (with the exception of the stable districts). Examination of their histories and local cultures led us to a very definite conclusion that the score differences were in no way the result of chance.

The 11 districts were bifurcated into either proactive, adaptive settings or change-resistant, reactive settings. Three communities showed proactive, responsive, adaptive, and innovative public instruction, and eight were in more or less severe states of inaction, factiousness, and confusion. Two of the three high-performing districts, Isaac and National, have included small ethnic and language minority subcommunities for two generations that gradually increased to become a majority of the population. The third district, Rosemead, was monocultural and ethnically homogeneous until the 1980s, but as it began to host large numbers of minority newcomers, it was exceptionally distinctive in its cultural predisposition to be positive, welcoming, and adaptive toward newcomers—a predisposition grounded in the Anglo political leadership.

High-performing districts tended to show a greater degree of social tolerance and respect for multicultural pluralism and inclusion values. They also demonstrated more familial harmony and placed a high value on public service.

## Organization

Analyses of the organizational structure, personnel commitments, and dynamic functioning of the districts and their schools within the larger system context of the states and communities disclosed several ways in which districts move, or fail to move, to assimilate rising numbers of disadvantaged students. Large population size was found to be a deterrent to effective functioning, especially in situations of rapid growth in short time periods. Very large size, when combined with district failure to adopt to population change and severe needs, is seen as fatal. The elements of success are too interdependent to be rank-ordered but are summarized here.

**Community Characteristics.** In successful districts we see a history of accommodating language minority groups and strong community support for the schools. Striking characteristics in these districts include a familial atmosphere, low levels of segregation, and an absence of strife. Parents are involved in school activities, are active on committees, and are not overwhelmed by fiscal or language problems.

**School Board.** Ethnic and language minority groups that have recently arrived are represented on the board, and veteran Anglo board members do not coalesce around opposition to program changes. Most board members agree strongly that the superintendent should be empowered to change the district's programs in order to host and educate newcomers effectively. They back the superintendent's efforts to do this and do not fight among themselves. Support for changes in policy and practice, combined with school visits by board members and their participation in the school lives of children and staff, are necessary features of board success.

**Superintendent.** The superintendents who succeed regard cultural diversity as a strength of their schools and are pragmatically very active in every aspect of their districts, while directing their influence and resources to a priority concern with serving disadvantaged children and youth. This priority, often best expressed in efforts to promote bilingual instruction that works, is carried out by successful superintendents through a wide and deep network of involvements that they pursue in district, statewide, and even national organizations. It is not the superintendent's gender, ethnicity, or socioeconomic background that distinguishes success from mediocrity and failure in serving disadvantaged minority students; rather, it is the superintendent's identification of that service as an imperative that matters most.

**Other Professional Staff.** Successful districts maintain small administrative staffs and invest their resources in pay, benefits, training opportunities, and support for teachers. Superintendents involve themselves directly in the selection of principals, assistant principals, and bilingual teachers. Those staff, in turn, are dedicated to very high levels of individual and team involvement in community relations and to long hours of extra effort within their school sites. They have a consensus on goals and priorities and support the superintendent.

**Authority and the Incentive System.** Staff in successful districts have the autonomy needed to do outstanding work within the constraints of a district policy commitment to instruction and child-centered service, and they express a strong sense of their empowerment. At the same time, they interact frequently, intensely, and trustingly with the central administration. Site-based management may, or may not, be the rhetoric used within the high-performing districts, and there are important variations in programs from building to building, but administrators and teachers in the successful districts share a common set of objectives to benefit disadvantaged learners.

Success is also strongly associated with the quality of leadership exerted by building principals. Every one of the 11 districts had some high-performing, professionally effective principals, but the 3 high-performing districts had principals of this caliber in nearly every building the field teams visited. These comparatively extraordinary educational leaders were observably intensely involved with teachers, custodians, parents, community volunteers, and colleagues at district headquarters. They were articulate, enthusiastic, and dedicated to the strengthening of their programs. Not only had they been selected because they could perform in this way, but also they were backed and celebrated by the superintendent and board members for their efforts.

### Health and Human Services

All of the districts suffer gravely from rising rates of crime, violence, drugs, and family breakdown. Isaac, the most harmonious district in the sample, held the record for the most drive-by shootings of any subcommunity of Phoenix in 1991, for example.

Even in the face of pressing problems, some communities and their schools are making a concerted effort to meet the needs of the children and their families. The high-performing districts differ sharply from others in the sample on the scope and quality of their provision of social, health, and psychological services for schoolchildren. Striking differences between high-performing and other districts are shown in the following ways: These districts display close collaboration between the schools and social and health agencies and police; have strong community support and involvement; integrate relations with diverse ethnic subcommunities; and, overall, make a much more pragmatically detailed, professionally aware investment in noneducational services than do other districts. Instead of debating about where public school help should be limited—for example, to instruction and schoolday security only—high-performing districts are unified and cooperative in their political determination to do what it takes to host and treat children and youth humanely and in ways that optimize their growth and life chances.

The differences are not explained solely by fiscal resources. What is available to invest locally is unmistakably important. Indeed, as the challenges facing youth intensify, fiscal resources for use by school districts will take on increasing importance. But, as we noted, some of the poorest districts in our sample did the most in providing good services, while some of the wealthiest did the least. Basically, our findings show that the differences in services provided to children relate to cooperation and support among different members of the community.

## IMPLICATIONS

A multiple-case comparison is limited in its ability to identify explanations for the pattern of differences between observed behaviors and documented events. Such a design can only verge on causal hypotheses, for example. This is especially so when the comparisons are grounded in one-time site visits, even when these include collection of historical trends. But comparative case analysis does permit elimination by reduction of some ideas that seem promising from the literature or from school lore, and case analysis also points toward some practices that have greater empirical credence than do others as sources of success in fostering achievement.

Three quite divergent interpretations of the nature and sources of achievement for disadvantaged students are contradicted by our findings. One of these has been fashionable since the Coleman report of 1966. It argues that family background determines achievement outcomes and that schools are of very limited importance in the process. A second theory is that the effect of structural dominance is so pervasive, leaving poor minorities shortchanged in so many ways, that total redistributive equity is needed before improvements in outcomes can be expected. And a third proposes that parental and individual student efforts to succeed—not the quality of what is provided by the schools—are what counts most.

The evidence from this study is that public school districts and their individual schools can, in fact, help to lift or depress student learning outcomes, even while socioeconomic, ethnic, and language minority status affect the process in their characteristically powerful way. We found that improvement in providing educational services to children hinges mainly upon local community or district politics, school organization, and instruction. There are communities in which schools make a great positive difference in the growth and life chances of the children, and this difference, doubtless affected one-by-one by differences in family relations and individual effort, can be organized and acted upon by communities intentionally.

Individual efforts, in other words, are often conditioned by local cultures and the quality of service delivered by educators. A newly arrived, poor, limited-English-proficient child in Isaac, Rosemead, or National may not be highly motivated or strongly supported by her family, for example, but she will be reinforced greatly in her efforts by the quality of teaching, health and protective services, and the comprehensive welcome she receives in contrast to the discouragement she would face in other school districts. She would, in effect, be provided with much greater opportunities to learn than her counterpart in low-performing districts would be.

The largest districts and the largest schools within them fared worse than the smallest districts in our sample. There was no qualitative evidence that contradicted the policy idea that, other things being equal, smaller is better in schooling. But our sample is far too small to support generalizations about district or school size, and it contains too few large districts. In addition, the literature—although it gives increasing credence to the smallness argument—also suggests that size may be a mere proxy variable for other organizational and program factors in public school districts.

This study cannot tell us whether the size of a school district's enrollment is determinative of success or failure. It does support the best current research literature, however, in suggesting that very large districts—those in excess of 15,000 perhaps—have a very difficult time succeeding if they are composed of proportionately large numbers of highly disadvantaged learners. Fresno is a case in point. Size in itself is not a cause of success or failure, but where poverty and minority status are present in high degrees, small districts probably have better prospects of organizing for success in their treatment of children. Our historical evidence suggests, moreover, that fractiousness, dissent, and bureaucratic pathologies tend to get built into big districts as they grow in size over time. It also suggests that the low-performing large districts were ineffective when they were much smaller, as well, and that the sources for this persist over generations.

The intervening factors this book examines in detail all influence the hosting and treatment of students. Each matters strongly. What matters far more, however, is their combination and organizational integration into a policy structure that defines the mission of the district. High-performing districts in our sample are distinguished by the ubiquitous presence of community and school system staff commitments to serve disadvantaged children and youth effectively.

We find that school districts can and do organize themselves to deliver excellent instruction in spite of the demographic odds to the contrary, and that districts can operate to offset the differences between levels of parental income. High-performing districts are generally ones in which the negative effects of poverty and immigrant status have been resisted by distinctive features of history and culture.

Instructional and related service program ingredients are widely understood by the hundreds of practitioners we interviewed. They are described by federal and state agencies, given special categorical funding from these agencies, and figure extensively in in-service training sessions focused on NEP and LEP instruction, whole-language approaches, hands-on science teaching, and so forth. Yet very few districts "turn the corner," so to speak, in concentrating their political will and financial resources on fostering and mounting an ever-growing and changing attack on the finite inequities of favoring some groups above others and on the challenges posed by poverty, family vulnerability, and the absence of culminating rewards for students who do their very best to beat the odds.

Our case reports show that a comprehensive, shared vision of the sort common to the high-performing districts can come into being under a variety of historical, cultural, and educational conditions. Isaac's vision, for example, evolved historically from events during World War II in its transformation from a semi-rural district on the far fringe of Phoenix to a truly urban, multi-ethnic district skilled in attracting external resources and proud of its ability to welcome and serve newcomers. In other words, Isaac benefited from having decades of practice in adapting its community and schools to great changes in demography, economy, and urbanization of the surrounding county.

National built its vision of success upon Anglo pride in the hospitality and multicultural goodwill of its historically homogeneous community. As Rosemead faced great challenges posed by the burgeoning Latino population during the 1980s, the district's decision makers chose with rather clear political preference to stress its inclusiveness and its determination to preserve and extend equal educational treatment to all students. In terms of political behavior, leaders made a choice between strengthening their power bases by urging neglect and avoidance of the newcomers or broadening the community's commitment to education by increasing outreach to new constituents. The latter course produced learning advantages for students.

Conversely, Sunnyside is a community in possibly terminal economic decline. That is, it may no longer be able to support a school district and will have to merge with more viable communities around it. Some other districts in our low-performing group are unlikely to pursue a vision of improved help for newcomers because they continue to be organized around the allocation of resources to the middle-class Anglo households who dominate their communities politically and economically. This is also true of the stable Washoe County and Clark County districts in Nevada.

A comprehensive vision of excellent schooling and service delivery for all children will tend, therefore, to emerge under certain conjecturally limited conditions. Federal and state reforms appear to us unlikely to generate those conditions. Traces of those reforms, including categorical program and project funding, appear in all of our sample districts but do not differentiate among them in their quality of functioning. If this is the case, transformative improvements in educational and related services for children hinge mainly upon local community politics, political culture, and school organization. It will matter greatly who runs for local office, who gets elected to the school board, and how these leaders choose, mandate, and then support a superintendent who reorganizes their district to make it comprehensively successful in hosting new generations of culturally diverse children.

Our comparisons suggest that the Coleman (1966) report was incorrect; that school districts can and sometimes do organize themselves to deliver excellent and pertinent instruction in spite of the demographic odds to the contrary. Similarly, our findings suggest that the structural dominance perspective is too deterministic; that countervailing organizational, instructional, and service delivery arrangements indeed emerge and are fostered in some communities.

Although little is known about how to engineer change in political cultures, this study makes a contribution to those community leaders, parents, and educators who are committed to improving the conditions that shape disadvantaged newcomers' opportunity to learn. Its contribution rests in identifying the features and practices that matter most.


## THE SOCIOLOGY OF IMPACTED SCHOOL DISTRICTS

This study has documented the many ways in which public school districts that undergo heavy increases in low-income minority students may organize their policies, resources, personnel, and programs of instruction and service to host those newcomers, as well as the "regular" students, effectively. That this is an uncommon process of adaptive change goes without saying. Most districts, impacted demographically or not, are shaped by their social, economic, and ethnic stratification patterns—patterns that tend to overdetermine which children will be school winners and which school losers.

The exceptional districts that succeeded in making this change give us fairly consistent and patterned approaches that can, at least hypothetically, be incorporated into thousands of other similarly challenged districts, as the income-related, language, and ethnic diversities of students expand during the 1990s and into the coming century in hundreds of the nation's metropolitan cities, towns, and suburbs. What is missing, we think, is not local access to ways of improving a community's public schools, nor is it the absence of both demographic and economic pressure to improve public school performance. It is, instead, the strong tendency of localities to adhere to long-rationalized traditions of advantagement of the few and indifference toward the many. As currents of political conservatism continue to rise, carrying with them antagonism toward newcomers, ill will toward the welfare poor, and a disposition to raise academic standards without corresponding raises in educational investments in children at risk, these traditions take on, at least for the short term, a glamour of their own.

The sociological question that persists, therefore, is how long the hegemony of structural dominance can continue before its consequences—the generation of a vast underclass, of rising rates of crime and violence, and of ever more imposing costs of social containment—become unbearable. The patterns of successful functioning we have identified and interpreted can be introduced without increased investments and with great benefits for the children of the socioeconomically advantaged as well as for the children of the poor.

Absent the adoption of this pattern, in fact, advantaged children's opportunities to learn will suffer, as they already do to a marked extent in the low-performing districts we studied. Vouchers and charter schools will not permit sufficient numbers of advantaged children to escape to settings where they will not be held as educational hostages to the anger and rising illiteracy of their peers. And the onset of privatization in a small handful of districts has been minimal and filled with setbacks.

We foresee a time, perhaps late in this decade or early in the next, when the pressure to adapt and the costs of persisting with the status quo will become too intense to be avoided. That time will converge with concurrent trends in the radical change of conventional child-rearing practices and supports. School districts, large or small, will come in quest of the patterns for hosting newcomers and for doing it well, and we hope our comparative cases will help to guide them in that quest.

# References

Allen, J. E., Jr. (1969). *Educational problems of the inner city* (background paper for the President's Committee on Mental Retardation). Presented at the Conference on Problems of Education of Children in the Inner City, Washington, DC.

Arizona State Department of Education. (1992). *State education profiles.* Phoenix, AZ: Author.

Baker, K. A., & de Canter, A. (1981). *The effectiveness of bilingual education: A review of the literature.* Washington, DC: U.S. Department of Education. (ERIC Document Reproduction Service No. ED 215 010)

Berlin, B., et al. (1989, March). *Organizational size and learning.* Paper presented at the annual meeting of the American Educational Research Association, San Francisco. (ERIC Document Reproduction Service No. ED 301 665)

Berman, P., Chamber, I., Gandara, P., McLaughlin, B., Minicucci, C., Nelson, B., Olsen, L., & Parish, T. (1992). *Meeting the challenges of language diversity: An evaluation of programs for pupils with limited proficiency in English. Volume 1: Executive Summary.* Berkeley, CA: BW Associates.

Birman, B., Orland, M.E., Jung, R., Anson, R., Garcia, G., Moore, M., Funkhouse, J., Morrison, D., Turnbull, B., & Reisener, E. (1987). *The current operation of the Chapter 1 Program.* Washington, DC: U.S. Department of Education.

Bloch, D., & Swadener, E. B. (1992). Children and families at risk: Etiology, critique and alternative paradigms. *Educational Foundations, 4*(4), 17–39.

Brophy, J., & Good, T. (1986). Teacher behavior and student achievement. In M. C. Wittrock (Ed.), *Handbook of research on teaching* (3rd ed.). New York: Macmillan.

Brown, D. J. (1992, September). The decentralization of school districts. *Educational Policy, 6*(3), 289–297.

California Commission on Teacher Credentialing. (1992). *Overview of the design for the preparation and credentialing of teachers for limited-English-proficient students.* Sacramento: Author.

California Department of Education. (1984). *Performance report for California's schools: Indicators of performance.* Sacramento: Author.

California Department of Education. (1992). *California task force report.* Sacramento: Author.

California Department of Education. (1993). *Handbook of education information fact sheet, 1992–93.* Sacramento: Author.

Casteneda, L. (1992). *Improving programs of schools serving culturally and linguistically diverse student populations: A review of the literature* (unpublished report). Los Alamitos, CA: Southwest Regional Laboratory.

Catterall, J. S. (1987). On the social costs of dropping out of school. *High School Journal, 71,* 19–30.

Center for the Study of Social Policy. (1992). *Kids count data book.* Washington, DC: Author.

Coleman, J. (1966). *Equality of educational opportunity.* Washington, DC: U.S. Government Printing Office.

Coleman, P., & LaRocque, L. (1988). *Reaching out: Instructional leadership in school districts.* Ontario, Canada: Simon Frasier University and Social Science and Humanities Research Council.

Collier, V. P. (1992). A synthesis of studies examining long term language minority student data on academic achievement. *Bilingual Research Journal, 16*(1 & 2), 187–212.

Corbett, H., & Rossman, G. B. (1988). *How teachers empower superordinates: Running good schools.* Philadelphia: Research for Better Schools.

Corwin, R. (1994). *Contrasting district practices: A profile of the high-performing school district* (unpublished report). Los Alamitos, CA: Southwest Regional Laboratory.

Cuban, L. (1984). Transforming the frog into a prince: Effective school research, policy and practice at the district level. *Harvard Educational Review, 54*(2), 129–151.

Cummins, J., & McNeely, S.N. (1987). Language development, academic learning and empowering minority students. In S. H. Fradd & W. J. Tikunoff (Eds.), *Bilingual education and bilingual special education* (pp. 75–98). Boston: Little, Brown.

Delgado-Gaitan, C., & Trueba, H. (1991). *Crossing cultural borders: Education for immigrant families in America.* Bristol, PA: The Falmer Press.

Dentler, R. A. (1984). Ambiguities in state-local relations. *Education and Urban Society, 16*(2), 145–164.

Dentler, R. A. (1987). The education of the baby boom generation. In R. G. Corwin (Ed.), *Research in sociology of education and socialization.* Greenwich, CT: JAI Press.

Dentler, R. A. (1992, October). The Los Angeles riots of spring 1992: Events, causes and future policy. *Sociological Practice Review, 3*(4), 229–244.

Dentler, R. A., Baltzell, D. C., & Chabotar, K. J. (1983). *Quality integrated magnet schools and their costs.* Cambridge, MA: Abt Associates.

Dianda, M. (1991). *New teachers in California's language diverse metropolitan classrooms: Findings from an initial study* (unpublished report). Los Alamitos, CA: Southwest Regional Laboratory.

Eisner, E. W. (1992). Educational reform and the ecology of schooling. *Teachers College Record, 93*(4), 610–627.

Elmore, R. F., & McLaughlin, M. W. (1988, February). *Steady work: Policy, practice, and the reform of American education.* Santa Monica, CA: RAND Corporation.

Embracing diversity. (1992, January 16). *Education Daily,* p. 1.

Espinosa, R. W., & Ochoa, A. M. (1992). *The educational attainment of California youth*: *A public equity crisis*. San Diego State University, Department of Policy Studies in Language and Cross Cultural Education.

Firestone, W. A. (1989). Using reform: Conceptualizing district initiatives. *Educational Evaluation and Policy Analysis, 11*(2), 151–164.

Friedkin, N. E., & Necochea, J. (1988). School system size and performance: A contingency perspective. *Educational Evaluation and Policy Analysis, 10*(3), 237–249.

Fullan, M. (1990). Staff development, innovation, and institutional development. In B. Joyce (Ed.), *Changing school culture through staff development: 1990 yearbook of the Association for Supervision and Curriculum Development*, 3–25. Alexandria, VA: Association for Supervision and Curriculum Development.

Fullan, M., & Pomfret, A. (1977). Research on curriculum and instruction implementation. *Review of Educational Research 5*(47), 335–397.

Gans, H. (1972). Foreword. In Colin Greer, *The great American school legend: A revisionist interpretation of American public education*. New York: Basic Books.

Garcia, E. E. (1992). *The education of linguistically and culturally diverse students: Effective instructional practices*. Washington, DC: Center for Applied Linguistics.

General Accounting Office (1995, September). *School finance: Trends in education spending* (Report No. B-259607). Washington, DC: U.S. Government Accounting Office.

Guskey, T. R., & Huberman, M. (Eds.). (1995). *Professional development in education: New paradigms and practices*. New York: Teachers College Press.

Hafner, A. L. (1993). Teaching method scale and math class achievement: What works with different outcomes? *American Educational Research Journal, 30*(1), 71–94.

Hafner, A. L., & Green, J. S. (1992). *Multicultural education and diversity: Providing information to teachers*. Paper presented at the Annual Meeting of the American Association of Colleges of Teacher Education, San Antonio, TX.

Hallinger, P., & Edwards, M. A. (1992). The paradox of superintendent leadership in school restructuring. *School Effectiveness and School Improvement, 3,* 131–149.

Hargreaves, A., & Dawe, R. (1989). *Coaching as unreflective practice*. Paper presented at the annual meeting of the American Educational Research Association, San Francisco.

Harry, B. (1992). *Cultural diversity, families and the special education system: Communication and empowerment*. New York: JC Press.

Healthy Start Support Services for Children Act, S.B. 620. (1993). Sacramento: California State Senate.

Hernandez, H. (1992). The language minority student and multicultural education. In Carl A. Grant (Ed.), *Research and multicultural education*. Bristol, PA: The Falmer Press.

Hirsh, S., & Sparks, D. (1991, September). A look at the new central office administrators. *School Administrator, 48*(7), 16–17.

Hoffer, T., Greeley, A., & Coleman, J. S. (1985). Achievement growth in public and Catholic schools. *Sociology of Education, 58,* 74–97.

Hollingshead, A. B. (1949). *Elmtown's youth: The impact of social classes on adolescents*. New York: Wiley.

Hollingshead, A. B. (1975). *Elmtown's youth and Elmtown revisited.* New York: Wiley.

Hord, S. M., Rutherford, W. L., Huling-Austin, L., & Hall, G. E. (1987). *Taking charge of change.* Alexandria, VA: Association for Supervision and Curriculum Development.

Howe, K. R. (1992). Liberal democracy, equal educational opportunity and the challenge of multiculturalism. *American Educational Research Journal, 29*(3), 455–470.

Howley, C. (1989, Fall). Synthesis of the effects of school and district size: What research says about achievement in small schools and school districts. *Journal of Rural and Small Schools, 4*(1), 2–12.

Jang, Y., & Mangione, P. (1993). *Transition program practices: Improving linkages between early childhood education and early elementary school* (unpublished report). Los Alamitos, CA: Southwest Regional Laboratory.

Jiobu, R. M. (1988). *Ethnicity and assimilation.* Albany, NY: State University of New York Press.

Jiobu, R. M. (1990). *Ethnicity and assimiliation: Blacks, Chinese, Filipinos, Koreans, Japanese, Mexicans, Vietnamese and Whites.* Albany, NY: State University of New York Press.

Justiz, M., & Kameen, M. (1988). Increasing the representation of minorities in the teaching force. *The Peabody Journal of Education, 66,* 91–100.

Knapp, M. S., & Shields, P. (1990). Reconceiving academic instruction for the children of poverty. *Phi Delta Kappan, 71*(10), 753–758.

Krashen, S., & Biber, D. (1988). *On course: Bilingual education's success in California.* Sacramento: California Association for Bilingual Education.

Lambert, M. (1991, November 26). Diverse teaching staffs urged: Workforce in state still largely white, legislative committee told. *Sacramento Bee,* p. A4.

Lee, V. (1986). *Multilevel causal models for social class and achievement.* Paper presented at the annual meeting of the American Educational Research Association, San Francisco.

Lee, V., & Bryk, A. (1988). A multi-level causal model of the social distribution of high school achievement. Unpublished paper.

Legarreta, D. (1977). Language choice in bilingual classrooms. *TESOL Quarterly, 11,* 9–16.

Little, J. (1982). Norms of collegiality and experimentation: Workplace conditions of school success. *American Educational Research Journal, 5*(19), 325–340.

Little, J. W., Gerritz, W. H., Stern, D. S., Guthrie, J. W., Kirst, M. W., & Marsh, D. (1987, December). *Staff development in California: Public and personal investments, program patterns, and policy choices.* San Francisco: Far West Laboratory for Educational Research and Development and Policy Analysis for California Education (PACE).

Loucks-Horsley, S., Harding, C. K., Arbuckle, M., Murray, L. B., Dubea, C., & Williams, M. K. (1987). *Continuing to learn: A guidebook for teacher development.* Andover, MA, & Oxford, OH: The Regional Educational Laboratory for Educational Improvement of the Northeast and Islands and National Staff Development Council.

Louis, K. S., Kell, D., & Dentler, R. A. (1984). *Exchanging ideas.* Cambridge, MA: Abt Associates.

Lueder, D. (1989). Tennessee parents were invited to participate: And they did. *Educational Leadership, 47*(2), 15–17.

Marshall, C., Mitchell, D. E., & Wirt, F. M. (1985). Assumptive worlds of education in policy makers. *Peabody Journal of Education, 62,* 90–115.

McDonnell, L. M., & Hill, P. (1993). *Newcomers in American schools.* Santa Monica, CA: RAND Corporation.

McLaughlin, M. W., Shepard, L. A., & O'Day, J. A. (1995). *Improving education through standards-based reform.* Stanford, CA: National Academy of Education.

Means, B., Chelemer, C., & Knapp, M. S. (Eds.). (1991). *Teaching advanced skills to at-risk students: Views from research and practice.* San Francisco: Jossey-Bass.

Merino, B. (1991). Promoting school success for Chicanos: The view from inside the bilingual classroom. In *Chicano School Failure and Success,* R. Valencia (Ed.). New York: Pergamon Press.

Miles, M. B., & Huberman, A. M. (1994*). Qualitative data analysis* (2nd ed.). Thousand Oaks, CA: Sage.

Miller, L. (1988). Unlikely beginnings: The district office as a starting point for developing a professional culture of teaching. In A. Lieberman (Ed.), *Building a professional culture in schools* (pp. 167–184). New York: Teachers College Press.

Monk, D. H. (1992). Modern conceptions of educational quality and state policy regarding small schooling units. In *Sourcebook on school and district size, cost and quality.* (ERIC Document Reproduction Service No. ED 361 160)

Montgomery, A. F., & Rossi, R. J. (1994). Becoming at risk of failure in America's schools. In R. J. Rossi (Ed.), *Schools and students at risk: Context and framework for positive change* (pp. 3–22). New York: Teachers College Press.

Mullin, S. P., & Summers, A. (1983). Is more better? The effectiveness of spending on compensatory education. *Phi Delta Kappan, 64,* 330–343.

Murnane, R. J., Singer, J. D., Willett, J. B., Kemple, J. J., & Olsen, R. J. (1991). *Who will teach: Policies that matter.* Cambridge, MA: Harvard University Press.

Natriello, G., McDill, E., & Pallas, A. (1990). *Schooling disadvantaged children: Racing against catastrophe.* New York: Teachers College Press.

Nel, J. (1992). The empowerment of minority students: Implications of Cummins' model for teacher education. *Action in Teacher Education, 14*(3), 38–45.

Nevada Department of Education. (1992). *State Profiles.* Reno: Author.

Oakes, J. (1985). *Keeping track: How schools structure inequality.* New Haven, CT: Yale University Press.

Oakes, J. (1990). *Multiplying inequalities.* Santa Monica, CA: RAND Corporation.

O'Day, J. A., & Smith, M. (1993). Systemic reform and educational opportunity. In S. Fuhrman (Ed.), *Designing coherent education policy* (pp. 250–313). San Francisco: Jossey-Bass.

Olsen, L., & Mullen, N. A. (1990). *Embracing diversity: Teachers' voices from California classrooms* (California Tomorrow Immigrant Students Project Research Report). San Francisco: California Tomorrow.

Persell, C. H. (1977). *Education and inequality: The roots and results of stratification in America's schools.* New York: Free Press.

Pink, W. (1989). *Effective development for urban school improvement.* Paper presented at the annual meeting of the American Educational Research Association, San Francisco.

Ramirez, J. D., et al. (1992). Executive summary. *Bilingual Research Journal,* 16(1 & 2), 1–62.

Rosenholtz, S. (1989). *Teachers' workplace.* New York: Longman.

Rothstein, S. W. (Ed.). (1993). *Handbook of schooling in urban America.* Westport, CT: Greenwood Press.

Rowley, S. R. (1992, April). *School district restructuring and the search for coherence: A case study of adaptive realignment and organizational change.* Paper presented at the annual meeting of the American Educational Research Association, San Francisco.

Rumberger, R., & Wilms, J. D. (1992). The impact of racial and ethnic segregation on the achievement gap in California high schools. *Educational Evaluation and Policy Analysis,* 14(4), 377–396.

Sacken, D. M., & Medina, M., Jr. (1990). Investigating the context of state-level policy formation: A case study of Arizona's bilingual educational legislation. *Educational Evaluation and Policy Analysis,* 12(4), 389–402.

Sarason, S. (1982). *The culture of the school and the problem of change* (2nd ed.). Boston: Allyn & Bacon.

Shanker, A. (1990). Staff development and the restructured school. In B. Joyce (Ed.), *Changing school culture through staff development: 1990 yearbook of the Association for Supervision and Curriculum Development* (pp. 91–103). Alexandria, VA: Association for Supervision and Curriculum Development.

Shavelson, R. J., McDonnell, L., Oakes, J., Carey, N., & Picus, L. (1987). *Indicator systems for monitoring math and science education.* Santa Monica, CA: RAND Corporation.

Slavin, R. E., Dolan, L., Madden, N. A., Karweit, N. L., & Wasik, B. A. (1992). *Success for All: Policy implications.* Baltimore: Johns Hopkins University, Center for Research on Effective Schooling for Disadvantaged Students.

Slavin, R. E., Karweit, N. L., & Madden, N. A. (1989). *Effective programs for students at risk.* Boston: Allyn & Bacon.

Snyder, T. D., & Hoffman, C. M. (1993). *Digest of educational statistics, 1993.* Washington, DC: National Center for Education Statistics.

Spellman, S. O. (1988, July–August). Recruitment of minority teachers: Issues, problems, facts, possible solutions. *Journal of Teacher Education,* 58–63.

Stevens, F. I. (1993). *Opportunity to learn: Issues of equity for poor and minority students.* Washington, DC: National Center for Education Statistics.

Stigler, J. (1990). *Mathematical knowledge of Japanese, Chinese, and American elementary school children.* Reston, VA: National Council of Teachers of Mathematics.

Stinnette, L. J. (1993). *Decentralization: Why, how and toward what ends?* (Special Policy Report No. 1, Policy Briefs Series). (ERIC Document Reproduction Service No. ED 368 047)

Swap, S. M. (1990). Comparing three philosophies of home–school collaboration. *Equity and Choice,* VI(3), 9–19.

Tropman, J. E. (1977). The constant crisis: Social welfare and the American cultural structure. In J. E. Tropman, M. Dluhy, & R. M. Lind (Eds.), *New strategies and perspectives on social policy* (pp. 7–29). New York: Pergamon Press.

U.S. Census Bureau. (1994). *School District Data Book.* Washington, DC: National Center for Education Statistics.

Walberg, H. J. (1992). On local control: Is bigger better? In *Sourcebook on school and district size, cost and quality.* (ERIC Document Reproduction Service No. ED 361 164)

Wehlage, G., Rutter, R., & Smith, M. (1989). *Reducing the risk: Schools as communities of support.* Bristol, PA: The Falmer Press.

Wills, F. G., & Peterson, K. D. (1992). External pressures for reform and strategy formation at the district level: Superintendents' interpretations of state demands. *Educational Evaluation and Policy Analysis, 14*(3), 241–260.

Winfield, L., Hawkins, R., & Stringfield, S. (1992, October). *A description of Chapter 1 schoolwide projects and effects on student achievement in six case study schools.* Baltimore: Center for Research on Effective Schooling for Disadvantaged Students.

Wright, R. (1996, June 12). U.S. child poverty worst among richest nations. *Los Angeles Times,* p. A22.

Yin, R. (1986). *Case study research.* Newbury Park, CA: Sage.

Young, K. (1977). Values in the policy process. *Policy and Politics, 5,* 1–22.

Zimmerman, S. (1992). *Family policy and family well being: The role of political culture.* Newbury Park, CA: Sage.

# APPENDIX:
# RATING SCALES

## General Instructions

A. Before you visit a school, review all the items in the rating scale.
B. During school visit(s) watch for and inquire into matters relevant to the items.
C. Within an hour after visiting a school, fill out your ratings on each of the statements. Use the 1–6 scale (1 = strongly disagree—6 = strongly agree).
D. If during your field work, you visit the same school on more than one occasion, adjust your ratings if needed after the last visit.
E. Each site team partner should fill out a sheet for each school visited.
F. During debriefing sessions, team members should discuss and agree on a joint team rating for each school visited.
G. Using the joint team sheet, add up the ratings to get a point total for each school visited.
H. Record the point total as indicated.
I. Divide the point total by the highest possible score on the scale and put the resulting overall score in the blank as indicated.
J. Attach the individual team member rating sheets to the joint team rating sheet (all ratings will be kept in the Mother File).

Use the following scale to rate how strongly you agree or disagree with each of the following statements about this school.  Do not leave blanks.

| 1 | 2 | 3 | 4 | 5 | 6 |
|---|---|---|---|---|---|
| Strongly Disagree | Mostly Disagree | Mildly Disagree | Mildly Agree | Mostly Agree | Strongly Agree |

## Quality of Education Scale

Circle One :        JOINT TEAM RATING   INDIVIDUAL RATING

Rater Name(s) : _____

Name of LEA : _____

Name of School : _____

Total of Rating Scale Points          _____ ÷ 96 = _____ Overall Score

_____ 1. Regular classroom instruction appears to involve high teacher expectations and standards for the students.

_____ 2. Student work is posted in the classrooms.

_____ 3. Student achievement or merit is visibly recognized in classroom and/or school building postings, or school announcements.

_____ 4. School improvement and/or individual student achievement is mentioned in bulletins or newsletters sent by school to parents.

_____ 5. A large proportion of the faculty remains on campus after the school day officially ends.

_____ 6. Teacher morale seems high.

_____ 7. Staff has devised multiple uses for equipment and space on campus.

_____ 8. Parents and other adult volunteers can be readily observed on campus aiding in instruction or tutoring.

_____ 9. Staff-student interactions are positive, supportive, respectful, and friendly.

_____ 10. Numerous upcoming events are posted on bulletin boards on campus.

_____ 11. Students appear comfortable and sociable with one another in the halls, on the grounds, and elsewhere on campus.

_____ 12. Students are actively engaged in cooperative learning

_____ 13. Student-to-student cross-age tutoring is in use.

_____ 14. Student peer tutoring is in use.

_____ 15. Students appear to have strong school spirit, or strong affection for the school.

___ 16. FOR ELEMENTARY SCHOOL: School involvement in providing role models or visiting speakers is clearly evident.
FOR JR., MIDDLE, or H.S:School involvement with career days and/or job mentoring activities is clearly evident.

### Quality of Integration Scale

Circle One :    JOINT TEAM RATING    INDIVIDUAL RATING

Rater Name(s) : _____

Name of LEA : _____

Name of School : _____

Total of Rating Scale Points _____ ÷ 78 = _____ Overall Score

____ 1. Racial-ethnic composition of teaching staff reflects racial-ethnic composition of student body.

____ 2. Excepting bilingual or ESL classes, racial-ethnic mix of students in classrooms reflects racial-ethnic composition of student body.

____ 3. Positions of Principal and Vice/Assistant Principal(s) are filled by African Americans, Asians, Latinos or Native Americans.

____ 4. Racial-ethnic mix of student body reflects the diversity of the community at large.

____ 5. Racial-ethnic minority and LEP students are promoted from one grade level to another at the same rate as are nonminority English-proficient students.

____ 6. Racial-ethnic minority and LEP students are suspended, expelled, or assigned to other schools at the same rate as are nonminority English-proficient students.

____ 7. School staff express a positive belief in the worth of different racial, ethnic, or cultural group experiences as a learning resource.

____ 8. When discussing expectations for student academic performance, school administrators and teachers do not express racial-ethnic characterizations or distinctions and do not link performance with race or ethnicity.

____ 9. When discussing expectations for student behavior, school administrators and teachers do not express racial-ethnic characterizations or distinctions and do not link behavior with race or ethnicity.

____ 10. The racial-ethnic mix of students at each ability group level or tracking level at this school reflects the racial-ethnic mix of the student body at large. (If neither ability groups nor tracks exist, rate at highest end of scale.)

____ 11. Groups of students taking study hall together, or participating in lab or resource room activities together, reflect the racial and ethnic mix of the student body at large.

____ 12. Groups of students participating in field trips, off-site competitions, etc., together reflect the racial and ethnic mix of the student body at large.

____ 13. The school has recruiting procedures to encourage/help assure participation of racial-ethnic and LEP minority students in a wide variety of school and extracurricular activities.

## Quality of Multiculturalism Scale

PLEASE NOTE: Only 2 of the 5 scales are designed to yield a different overall score for elementary schools versus other schools.

Circle One :        JOINT TEAM RATING    INDIVIDUAL RATING

Rater Name(s) : _____

Name of LEA : _____

Name of School : _____

Total of Elementary Rating Scale Points     ____ ÷ 132 = ____ Overall Score.
Total of Middle, Jr., or H.S. Scale Points     ____ ÷ 150 = ____ Overall Score.

____ 1. ESL and Bilingual classes are offered.

____ 2. LEP and NEP students receive native-language support.

____ 3. Students are able to receive content-area tutoring in native language.

____ 4. LEP students receive peer tutoring from bilingual students or other LEP students with greater English proficiency.

____ 5. Bilingual teachers or aides are available to or are teamed with class-room teachers who need help communicating with their LEP students.

____ 6. Posters, announcements, and invitations to participate in activities or events are bilingual / multilingual.

____ 7. Communications sent by school to parents are bilingual / multilingual.

____ 8. Translators are available on parent nights, for parent-teacher conferences, and at PTA or PTO meetings.

____ 9. If an LEP parent calls the school, a translator is generally available.

____ 10. Teachers and other staff can be heard speaking languages other than English.

____ 11. A multicultural curriculum committee provides / provided input into instructional materials.

____ 12. Multicultural instructional materials are plainly visible in the classroom at all grade levels.

____ 13. Posters, announcements, and invitations to participate in activities or events visually or topically reflect a diverse population.

____ 14. School celebrations, events, and commemorations reflect a diverse population.

____ 15. School library or resource room includes holdings in languages other than English.

____ 16. During student leisure time (e.g., recess and lunch in elementary school or changing classes and lunch in H.S., etc.), diverse groups of students are playing, talking, walking together.

____ 17. Classroom seating and group work arrangements do not segregate ethnic or linguistic minorities (other than for native-language support and ESL instruction).

____ 18. Extracurricular activities and student clubs (excluding national heritage and ethnic clubs) have diverse student membership/participation.

____ 19. Bulletin boards featuring student photos, newsclippings about students, student achievements or honors, etc., reflect diverse student population.

____ 20. Diversity is spoken of in positive terms rather than as a "problem" by school personnel.

____ 21. Teachers have received training in multicultural awareness.

____ 22. LEA and/or school code of conduct includes an official stance and/or rules against hate crime.

END OF SCALE ITEMS FOR ELEMENTARY SCHOOLS. RATE NEXT THREE ITEMS FOR MIDDLE, JUNIOR, OR HIGH SCHOOLS ONLY.

____ 23. National heritage and ethnic clubs exist on campus.

____ 24. ESL and bilingual classes are integrated with foreign language courses.

____ 25. Foreign language study is required for graduation.

## Quality of Organization Scale

Circle One :        JOINT TEAM RATING    INDIVIDUAL RATING

Rater Name(s): _____

Name of LEA: _____

Name of School: _____

Total of Rating Scale Points _____ ÷ 84 = _____ Overall Score

_____ 1. Tutoring and other instructional support are offered before, during, or after school.

_____ 2. Ability grouping is generally not used, except temporarily within classes for particular skill work.

_____ 3. Textbooks have recent (1985 or later) publication dates.

_____ 4. The school has special centers or laboratory facilities and equipment available for reading, math, language, and student computer learning.

_____ 5. The school curriculum includes art and provides arts materials for the students.

_____ 6. The school curriculum includes music and provides practice rooms and instruments for the students.

_____ 7. In-service training sessions or workshops are regularly scheduled for teachers to share techniques and/or materials.

_____ 8. At least one staff member is assigned *full-time* responsibility as parent or community liaison.

____ 9. At least one staff member is assigned *part-time* responsibility as parent or community liaison.

___ 10. Parent-teacher conferences are held regularly.

___ 11. The PTA is active in the school.

___ 12. Citizen Advisory Committees (other than the PTA) are active in the school.

___ 13. Newsletters, bulletins for the parents, and/or other communications from school to home are clearly evident.

___ 14. Observed student misconduct or behavioral problems seem well-handled and resolved.

## Quality of Teaching Scale

PLEASE NOTE: Only 2 of the 5 scales are designed to yield a different overall score for elementary versus other schools.

Circle One :     JOINT TEAM RATING   INDIVIDUAL RATING

Rater Name(s) : _____

Name of LEA : _____

Name of School : _____

Total of Elementary Rating Scale Points  _____ ÷ 84 = _____ Overall Score

Total of Middle, Jr., or H.S. Scale Points  _____ ÷ 96 = _____ Overall Score

____ 1. Teachers at this school press students to achieve academically.

____ 2. Students are expected to do homework (after grade 3).

____ 3. Counselors and teachers encourage students to enroll in academic classes.

____ 4. Teachers use a variety of teaching strategies or models, and a wide range of teaching materials.

____ 5. The school provides support for teachers' in-service education in the content area (e.g., release time).

_____ 6. Teachers are given incentives to increase their knowledge and pedagogical skills in the content area.

_____ 7. Teacher make an effort to coordinate the content of their course with other teachers.

_____ 8. School administrators and/or area coordinators are supportive and encouraging when teachers want to try out new ideas.

_____ 9. There is visible/apparent cooperation among staff members.

_____ 10. Teachers are familiar with the content and goals of courses taught by other teachers in their department or curricular area.

_____ 11. Teachers talk with one another about their teaching techniques, materials, and/or students.

_____ 12. Teachers believe their success in teaching students is due primarily to their own ability.

_____ 13. Teachers perceive many students are capable of learning the material.

_____ 14. Teachers feel it is worthwhile to try to do their best.

END OF SCALE ITEMS FOR ELEMENTARY SCHOOLS. RATE NEXT TWO ITEMS FOR MIDDLE, JUNIOR, OR HIGH SCHOOLS ONLY.

_____ 15. Alternative assessment sources such as journals, portfolios, or other criterion measures are used in student grading, placement, or promotion.

_____ 16. This school provides broad learning opportunities to students such as science or math fairs, subject matter clubs, computer lab, etc.

# Index

# About the Authors

Robert A. Dentler is Professor Emeritus of Sociology at the University of Massachusetts at Boston. A specialist in the sociology of education, Dr. Dentler has been a Senior Scientist at the Southwest Regional Laboratory, Manager of Educational Research at Abt Associates Inc., Dean of Education at Boston University, Director of the Center for Urban Education and Professor of Sociology and Education at Teachers College, Columbia University. He is author or co-author of 12 books and more than 100 articles.

Anne L. Hafner is an Associate Professor in the Charter School of Education at California State University at Los Angeles. A specialist in teaching and learning, methodology and assessment, she received her Ph.D. at UCLA in Educational Psychology. Dr. Hafner has been a researcher at UCLA's Center for the Study of Evaluation and at Southwest Regional Laboratory, and served as a statistician with the National Center for Education Statistics in Washington, DC. She is author or co-author of several books and numerous articles and reports.